Red Line 6

Standardaufgaben

von
Rachel Teear
Jenny Wood

sowie
Pauline Ashworth
Jennifer Baer-Engel
Bernadette Kesting

Ernst Klett Verlag
Stuttgart • Leipzig

Red Line 6 Standardaufgaben

Zeichenerklärung:
- Übungen mit diesem Symbol verweisen auf die CD zum Hörverstehen.

Audio-CD

Aufnahmeleitung: Ernst Klett Verlag GmbH, Stuttgart
Redaktion: Lektorat editoria, Cornelia Schaller, Fellbach
Aufgenommen in Q Sound, London
Aufnahme: Tim Woolf
Produktion: John Green, TEFL Tapes
Sprecherinnen und Sprecher:
Melissa Collier; Nicole Davies; Tom Giles; James Goode;
John Hasler; Nils Hognestad; Harriet Kershaw; Paul Lincoln;
Kate Lock; Rachael Miller; Tania Rodrigues
Tontechnik: Tim Woolf
Presswerk: Optimal Media Produktion, Röbel / Müritz

Gesamtzeit: 46'08"

1. Auflage   1 5 4 3 2 1 | 2015 2014 2013 2012 2011

Alle Drucke dieser Auflage sind unverändert und können im Unterricht nebeneinander verwendet werden. Die letzte Zahl bezeichnet das Jahr des Druckes.

Das Werk und seine Teile sind urheberrechtlich geschützt. Das Gleiche gilt für die Software sowie das Begleitmaterial. Jede Nutzung in anderen als den gesetzlich zugelassenen oder in den Lizenzbestimmungen (CD) genannten Fällen bedarf der vorherigen schriftlichen Einwilligung des Verlags. Hinweis zu § 52 a UrhG: Weder das Werk noch seine Teile dürfen ohne eine solche Einwilligung eingescannt und in ein Netzwerk eingestellt werden. Dies gilt auch für Intranets von Schulen und sonstigen Bildungseinrichtungen. Fotomechanische oder andere Wiedergabeverfahren nur mit Genehmigung des Verlags.

© und ℗ Ernst Klett Verlag GmbH, Stuttgart 2011
Alle Rechte vorbehalten.
www.klett.de

Autoren: Rachel Teear, Lappersdorf; Jenny Wood, Bristol
sowie Pauline Ashworth, Stuttgart; Jennifer Baer-Engel, Göppingen; Bernadette Kesting, Breitenworbis
Redaktion: Lektorat editoria, Cornelia Schaller, Fellbach
Gestaltung: Wiebke Hengst, Ostfildern
Umschlaggestaltung: Koma Amok, Stuttgart
Umschlagfoto: Avenue Images GmbH (Banana Stock), Hamburg
Illustrationen: Simone Pahl, Berlin

Bildquellennachweis
Cover vorn Avenue Images GmbH RF (Bananastock), Hamburg; **8.1** iStockphoto (Steven Wynn), Calgary, Alberta; **12.1** shutterstock (Andrew Chin), New York; **12.2** shutterstock (adam.golabek), New York; **12.3** Fotolia LLC (Gladwin), New York; **12.4** Geoatlas, Hendaye; **12.5** Fotolia LLC (vospalej), New York; **12.6** Fotolia LLC (tony4urban), New York; **15.1** shutterstock (Caitlin Mirra), New York; **18.1** Ullstein Bild GmbH (iT), Berlin; **20.1** Alamy Images (newsphoto), Abingdon, Oxon; **24.1** shutterstock (Milosz Aniol), New York; **26.1** Getty Images (Lonely Planet Images/Alain Evrard), München; **27.1** shutterstock (Paul Prescott), New York; **30.1** shutterstock (Jack Qi), New York; **31.1** Wikimedia Foundation Inc. (PD), **St. Petersburg FL; 34.1** shutterstock (Entertainment Press), New York; **34.2** Getty Images (FilmMagic), München; **34.3** Getty Images, München; **39.1** Avenue Images GmbH (Image Source/RF), Hamburg; **Cover hinten** Avenue Images GmbH RF (Bananastock), Hamburg

Sollte es in einem Einzelfall nicht gelungen sein, den korrekten Rechteinhaber ausfindig zu machen, so werden berechtigte Ansprüche selbstverständlich im Rahmen der üblichen Regelungen abgegolten.

Druck: AZ Druck und Datentechnik GmbH, Kempten/Allgäu

Printed in Germany
ISBN 978-3-12-581164-5

Inhalt

Topic 1	4
Topic 2	16
Topic 3	26
Topic 4	35

Anhang:

Übersicht über die Aufgabentypen	44
Lösungen mit HV-Texten	46
Inhalt Audio-CD und Systemvoraussetzungen...	U3

Topic 1 A global language

1 Listening: Skype

Sven is talking to Merve, a Turkish girl who lives in Germany. Listen to their conversation.

a) Are the statements right or wrong? Tick.

	right	wrong
1. Sven is talking to Merve on the phone.		
2. Sven has a camera on his computer.		
3. Merve chats to lots of people on the Internet.		
4. Sven lives in the north of Sweden.		
5. Merve doesn't think Sven's English is very good.		
6. Merve is a native speaker of English.		
7. Her father is a basketball coach.		
8. Merve learnt her manga techniques in the USA.		
9. Sven used to animate[1] characters for his sister.		
10. He says he will help Merve with some animés.		

b) Answer the questions in complete sentences.

1. What did Sven do every day in the north of Sweden?

   _____

2. Where did his family live before they moved to the north of Sweden?

   _____

3. What did his parents do when they got to the north of Sweden?

   _____

c) What does Sven say about Sweden? Complete the sentences with the missing words.

Lots of people from all over the world go on (1) _____ to the north of Sweden. They go there in the (2) _____ to go cross-country skiing[2] and in the summer they (3) _____ hiking or fishing. In Sweden almost all films are (4) _____ in English.

d) What does Merve say she likes or thinks is good? Tick the correct boxes.

☐ using Skype   ☐ living in Sweden   ☐ her English
☐ films in English   ☐ cinemas in Germany   ☐ the USA
☐ Sven's animés   ☐ Sven making his sister laugh ☐ the Internet

[1]to animate ['ænɪmeɪt] – *animieren*, [2]cross-country skiing [ˌkrɒskʌntri 'skiːɪŋ] – *Langlauf*

2 Reading: About the English language

English is the lingua franca in many parts of the world and in many parts of life; science, business, and media, for example. This is because Britain played an important role globally from the 18th to the 20th century and since the beginning of the 20th century the USA has helped to keep English important.

But how did the English language develop[1]? It started in the fifth century when settlers[2] came to England from Northern Europe. 'Old English', as it is now called, developed from their language. Words like *ship*, *that* and *bath* come from this time. English never stayed the same, however; it changed as people from different northern countries attacked and came to live in England and brought their own language, Norse, with them. For example, the Vikings[3] attacked England in the 9th century and brought words like *sky* and *leg*. The biggest change, however, happened in the 11th and 12th centuries when England was attacked by the Normans[4]. After the Norman Conquest[5] a Norman, William the Conqueror, became King of England. From then on the richer and more powerful people spoke French while the rest of the people spoke English.

Then things began to change and many French words came into the English language. 10,000 French (or Norman) words came into the English language at this time, for example *prison* and *prince*. This is one reason why there are so many words and so many synonyms in English. Some words with the same or a similar meaning have a German origin and some have a French origin. For example, *flower* comes from the French *fleur*, and *bloom*, which is also a word for a flower, comes from the German *Blume*. Most English words came from other languages but there are many words that were made up. Shakespeare made up lots of new words (sometimes from other words) or used old words for new things. For example, Shakespeare gave us the words *lonely*, *hurry* and *excellent*. But we have no idea where some words, like *dog* and *fun* came from.

In the past lots of new words have been added to the English language, for example during World War I and II. *Shampoo* came from India from a Hindi word, *potato* from Haitian, and *slogan* from Gaelic. Many Latin[6] and Greek words came into English, too, but most of them came via a different language and often the meaning changed, along the way. For example, the words *disk*, *dish*[7] and *desk* all come from the Latin word 'discus' but they came into the English language at different times and in different ways.

English is still changing today. Some people say that about 25,000 new words come into the English language every year, but it is difficult to say exactly how many because there is no official definition of English – unlike for the German or French languages. Many new words come into English from other languages, for example, *kindergarten* and *kitsch* from German. People also need new words when new things are invented, for example, laptop or DVD player.

Not only is the vocabulary of English changing but also the grammar, and new expressions are entering all the time, too. Sometimes these expressions come from different types of slang. Many groups of people have their own slang. One famous type of slang is Cockney which comes from East London. They use expressions which rhyme with a word, for example, '*loaf of bread*'[8] means *head*. So if somebody says, "Use your loaf", they mean "use your head" or "think".

---

[1]to develop [dɪˈveləp] – *entwickeln*, [2]settler [ˈsetlə] – *Siedler/-in*, [3]Viking [ˈvaɪkɪŋ] – *Wikinger*, [4]Norman [ˈnɔːmən] – *Normanne*, [5]conquest [ˈkɒŋkwest] – *Eroberung*, [6]Latin [ˈlætɪn] – *Latein*, [7]dish [dɪʃ] – *Gericht (Essen)*, [8]loaf of bread [ˌləʊf əv ˈbred] – *Brotlaib*

1 Reading

a) Complete the mind map with the missing information.

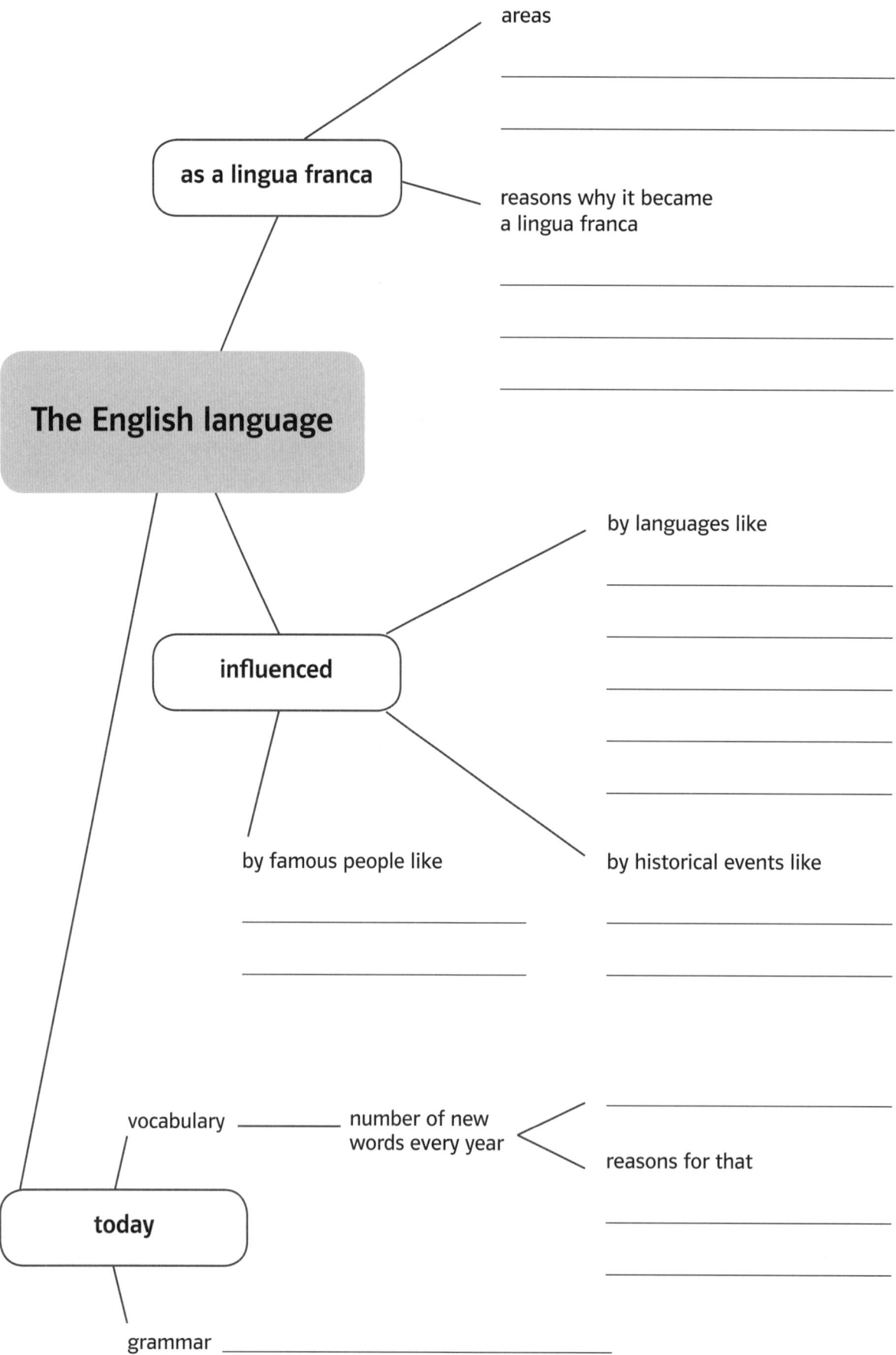

Reading 1

b) *Complete the grid with the missing facts. You needn't write full sentences.*

time	What happened?/ What influenced the English language?	new words that were added to the language
	settlers from Northern Europe, Old English developed	
Shakespeare's time		

c) *Explain why the English language is so rich in words and why there are so many synonyms.*

_____

_____

_____

_____

d) *What sort of text is it? Tick the best box.*

The text …
1. has a scientific[1] character and explains the influence of other languages on English in great detail. ☐
2. informs us about the history of the English language in a popular way so that readers can understand it easily. ☐
3. seems to be taken from a children's book and tells kids about the changes in the English language in a very simple and entertaining way. ☐

[1]scientific [ˌsaɪənˈtɪfɪk] – *wissenschaftlich*

1 Language

3 Revision: Past or present?

Put in the right present or past tense.

1. People _____ (speak) English all over the world since the 18th century.

2. Settlers from Northern Europe _____ (bring) their language to England in the 5th century.

3. Old English _____ (develop) from this language, but nobody _____ (use) it today.

4. William the Conqueror became King in the 11th century after he _____ (attack) England.

5. Then English slowly _____ (begin) to use some French words, too.

6. After the 17th century, people used words written by Shakespeare that _____ (not even exist) before.

7. Every time England _____ (come) into contact with other cultures, new words _____ (enter) the English language.

8. English grammar and vocabulary _____ (still change) all the time.

4 who, which or whose?

Put in the right relative pronoun.

English, _____ is a lingua franca in many parts of the world, is spoken in many areas of life. Modern English developed from the language of settlers _____ came to England from Northern Europe in the fifth century. The Normans, _____ leader was William the Conqueror, attacked England in the 11th century. The Normans introduced many French words _____ are still used today. English also has words _____ come from German and from many other countries _____ the English have attacked or lived in. One surprising fact is that Shakespeare, _____ is famous for his plays, just made up words or used old words _____ meaning he changed.

5 Comparatives and superlatives

Jane is talking to Dave about English. Choose the right adjective or adverb from the boxes and put it in the comparative or superlative form.

amazed   hot   fluent   good   arrogant   common   important   important   obvious

Jane: I've been reading about the English language. It's really interesting, and I was

_____ that we have so many words from other languages.

I hadn't really noticed.

Dave: Well, that's _____ to me. I mean, Britain's the

_____ country in the world, isn't it?

Jane: No, it's not. OK, it's _____ than, say, Tasmania, but …

Dave: So English is clearly the _____ language.

Jane: But isn't Chinese …?

Dave: So English must be the _____. And, look, many Indians speak

English, too.

Jane: Yes, but we've got a lot of words from India, too.

Dave: No, we haven't. They speak English, don't they, and they speak it

_____ than you do sometimes!

Jane: Well … what about curry? That's from India.

Dave: Hey, have you ever eaten a vindaloo? It's the _____ curry you

can get. But anyway, believe me, English is Number 1.

Jane: Do you know, Dave, you're the _____ person I've ever met.

6 Speaking: A phone call for a job

Situation: You want to get a job in the UK after your final exams. You see an ad for a software company in a British newspaper and call the firm to ask about it.
Write down your part of the phone call.

Ms Peters: Smith and Jones Software Ltd., Marion Peters speaking, how can I help you?

You: _____

_____

_____

_____

Begrüße Frau Peters und stelle dich vor. Sage, dass du ihre Annonce in der heutigen Zeitung gesehen hast und dass du dich um einen Job in ihrem Unternehmen bewerben möchtest.

1 Speaking

Ms Peters:	I see. Have you worked a lot with computers?	
You:	_____	Bejahe und sage, dass Informationstechnologie dein Lieblingsfach in der Schule ist.
Ms Peters:	Oh, you're still at school?	
You:	_____	Bejahe, aber erwidere, dass deine Abschlussprüfung im nächsten Monat stattfindet.
Ms Peters:	Can I ask where you come from?	
You:	_____	Sage, woher du in Deutschland kommst und dass du gern im Ausland arbeiten würdest, besonders im Vereinigten Königreich.
Ms Peters:	So English isn't your mother tongue?	
You:	_____	Entschuldige dich und bitte sie höflich, die Frage zu wiederholen.
Ms Peters:	Yes, er … aren't you fluent in English?	
You:	_____	Verneine die Frage und sage, dass du Englisch nicht sehr gut kannst. Dann korrigiere dich und sage, dass du Englisch doch sprechen kannst, aber dass du manchmal Fehler machst.
Ms Peters:	Well, that's no problem. You will learn a lot if you work here. Which job are you interested in?	
You:	_____	Sage, dass du gern im Team arbeitest und dass du dich für eine Stelle als Bürogehilfe/-gehilfin interessieren würdest.
Ms Peters:	Well, just fill in the application form which you can download from our website and we'll see what we can do for you.	
You:	_____	Bedanke dich sehr dafür, dass sie sich Zeit für dich genommen hat.
Ms Peters:	You're welcome. Goodbye.	

7 Writing: Application form

This is the application form you have downloaded from the website which Ms Peters told you about. Fill it in in note form.

Name:	
Address:	
Telephone:	
E-mail:	
Nationality:	
Education:	
Work experience:	
Job at the moment:	
Position you are applying for:	
Special skills:	
Personality¹:	
Good things about you:	
Things you could improve:	
Family:	
Goal(s):	
One more thing I would like people to know about me:	

¹personality [ˌpɜːsnˈæləti] – *Persönlichkeit, Charaktereigenschaften*

1 Listening

8 Listening: English speakers from around the world

You are going to hear Sebastian and five other participants of the Animé Summer Camp. Sebastian is from Germany but where do the other people come from?

a) *Draw lines to match the persons with the right flags.*

b) *Then put the name of the right country under each flag.*

9 Synonyms and definitions

Read the definitions and synonyms and put in the right words.

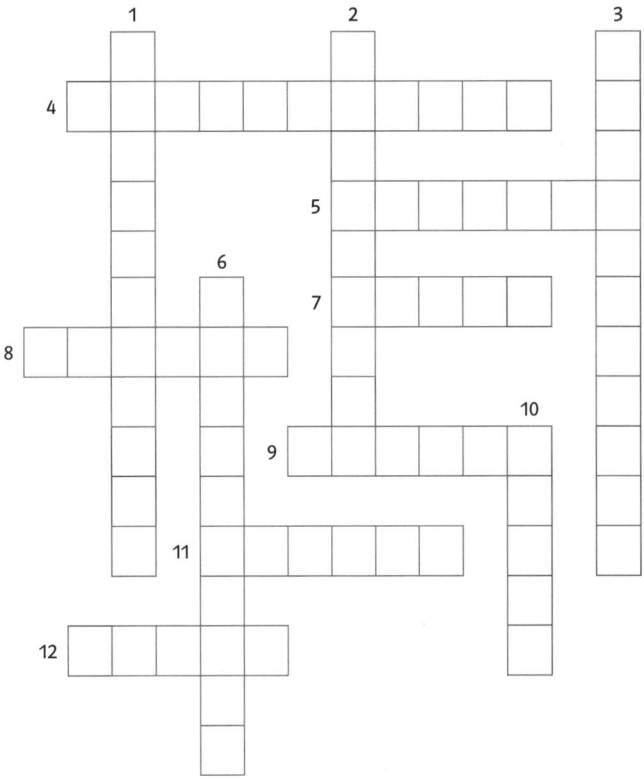

Down: ↓
1. word to describe what country you come from
2. sb who speaks two languages fluently
3. person who asks you questions when you have applied for a job
6. sb who doesn't eat meat
10. a test

Across: →
4. sb who takes part in sth
5. to add (to a letter or an e-mail)
7. the person in clue 8 might buy or sell these
8. sb who buys and sells things
9. you are this if you speak a language easily and well
11. very surprised
12. very fast

10 Find the opposites

Find the opposite pairs of words and write them down. Be careful – there are more words than you need!

future   final   first   later   leave out   like   mother tongue   immediately
search   bath   unlike   include   non-official
shower   past   request   backpacker   official   foreign language

_____ ≠ _____   _____ ≠ _____

_____ ≠ _____   _____ ≠ _____

_____ ≠ _____   _____ ≠ _____

_____ ≠ _____   _____ ≠ _____

1 Wordwise – Writing

11 Word families

Look at the words in the boxes and find a word from the same word family that fits in the text. You may need a dictionary for some words.

> emigration   mix   hope   fluency   major   immerse
> profession   passionate   talent

Hi, my name's Jean-Michel. I was born in France but my family _____ to the USA when I was five and I went to an _____ school in the USA for eight years. It's a great school. We had all our lessons in English and German, so now I'm _____ in both languages – and in French, of course. The _____ of the students were American, but there were three or four kids from Mexico, some from China, a few from Canada, and one guy from Africa, so it was a real _____ of nationalities. My favourite subject was sport. And American football is my _____! We had a _____ coach – he was a coach for the Minnesota Vikings for ten years before he came to our school – and he told me I was very _____ and could go far! It's great to be good at something, even if you are _____ at Math!

12 Writing: Your opinion

1. Which language will be the most common language in the world in 2050?
   Answer the question. Give reasons for your opinion.
   You may think of the following aspects:
   - whether English will still be the most commonly spoken and written language,
   - what changes in the English language may take place in the future,
   - what other languages may become important and/or
   - if there will even be one global language one day.

   Write in your exercise book.

   OR

2. *Bilingual lessons*

   More and more schools in Germany teach bilingually. And not only traditional subjects like Geography or History are taught in English or French, also Art or PE.
   Would you like to have bilingual PE lessons, too?
   Write a text and answer the question. Think of the advantages and disadvantages. Give reasons for your opinion.

   Write in your exercise book.

13 Mediation: The official language in the US

Situation: Du hast irgendwo gehört, dass die deutsche Sprache nach Gründung der USA beinahe zur Landessprache dort geworden wäre und dass mit nur einer Stimme Mehrheit die Entscheidung zugunsten von Englisch ausfiel. Du findest im Internet einen Artikel, der sagt, dass es sich dabei um eine Legende handelt.

German the official US language? Did German lose against English by just one vote?

Independence Hall in Philadelphia, Pennsylvania

The legend usually goes something like this: In 1776 English won over German by just one vote and English became America's official language instead of German.
It is a story that Germans, German teachers and many other people like to tell. But is it true?

At first glance[1] it may sound possible. Germans have always played an important role in US history. But a closer look shows several serious problems with this "official language" story. First of all the United States has never had an "official language" – English, German or any other – and it doesn't have one now. And there was never any such vote in 1776.
In 1795 US Congress debated[2] on languages, and a vote on German probably took place in 1795, but this vote dealt with translating US laws into German.
A few months later, however, the idea to publish[3] laws in languages other than English was dropped.
It is likely that the legend of German as the official language of the US started in the 1930s. Scientists think that the legend was part of the German-American Bund propaganda by the Nazis and aimed at[4] giving the German language more weight and importance in the world. By mixing this wish with certain[5] historical events in Pennsylvania, the German-American Bund probably produced this "national vote" story.

[1]glance [glɑːns] – *Blick*, [2]to debate [dɪˈbeɪt] – *debattieren*, [3]to publish [ˈpʌblɪʃ] – *veröffentlichen*, [4]to aim at [eɪm] – *abzielen auf*, [5]certain [ˈsɜːtn] – *gewisse*

1. Nenne die zwei Hauptargumente, die beweisen, dass es sich um eine Legende handelt.

2. Auf welchen tatsächlichen historischen Begebenheiten könnte die Legende basieren?

3. Welche Ereignisse nach 1930 trugen möglicherweise zur Entstehung und Verbreitung der Legende bei?

Topic 2 Change it!

1 Listening: Changing the world

a) *Read the sentences. Then listen and tick the <u>four</u> correct boxes.*

Emma ...	
1. is scared because a teenager has been killed.	☐
2. sometimes goes to council meetings.	☐
3. has read about violent school gangs in the paper.	☐
4. thinks that young people are responsible for things that go wrong.	☐
5. is shocked that teenagers have been killed by other teenagers.	☐
6. thinks James would be a good politician.	☐
7. thinks politicians can change a lot.	☐
8. always votes in elections.	☐

James ...	
1. says that only kids in gangs get killed.	☐
2. is in a political youth group.	☐
3. works with school gangs.	☐
4. thinks Emma's grandad is right.	☐
5. thinks the government should spend less on education.	☐
6. wants to be Prime Minister one day.	☐
7. thinks that one of society's biggest problems is that teenagers can't vote.	☐
8. thinks it is a good idea for Emma to be a singer.	☐

b) *Find the missing words and complete the text.*

The members of the political youth group sometimes go to (1) _____

meetings so they find out what's happening. They talk about how they could improve

things and sometimes work on (2) _____. Some people think that

teenagers who have got nothing better to do should (3) _____ _____ go in

the army for a year or two, because people learn things in the army and it would stop them

(4) _____ _____ street corners. Others think that

(5) _____ can't change things anyway. They just talk a lot about what

they are going to do when they win the election; then they win and do the opposite. Others say

that that happens sometimes, but that's because we live in a (6) _____.

c) *Tick the correct box.*

Emma and James ...
1. agree with each other most of the time. ☐
2. both want to improve the world. ☐
3. think politics is interesting. ☐

2 Reading: Queen of the United Kingdom, Canada, Australia, New Zealand and many more

Queen Elizabeth II is, as most people know, Queen of England but, as many people don't know, she is also Queen of the United Kingdom (England, Scotland, Wales and Northern Ireland) and Queen of 15 other countries: Australia, New Zealand, Canada, Jamaica, the Bahamas, Barbados, Grenada, St Christopher and Nevis, St Lucia, the Solomon Islands, Tuvalu, St Vincent and the Grenadines, Papua New Guinea, Antigua and Barbuda and Belize. What does that mean? And what powers does she have? And where are these countries anyway?

In Great Britain she is the Head of State and she has to open and dissolve Parliament[1], sign laws, and sign legal documents with other countries. The Queen has no real power in Great Britain, but what about in the other countries? How do Australians feel about the fact that their Head of State is the Queen of England? In Australia the Queen is called Queen of Australia. She is officially the Head of State but actually this job is done for her by the Governor-General[2] of Australia. The Queen's main duty is to officially name the Governor-General and the Governors of all the States, but she does not choose them.

The Prime Minister chooses the Governor-General and the States choose the Governors and then advise[3] the Queen. The Queen then names the Governors officially. The Australian Parliament has three parts: the Queen, the Senate and the House of Representatives. At the Opening of Parliament, the Queen or the Governor-General read 'The Speech from the Throne'. This speech is written by the government, as in Great Britain, and says what the Government plans to do that year. Though the Queen has the power to stop laws in Australia, she actually would not be allowed to do this. The Queen or members of the Royal Family visit Australia quite often for important events – for Australia Day, for example, or to open the Olympics. The Queen has visited Australia 15 times. So what do Australians think of all this? As you would expect, some Australians like it and some do not. In 1999 there was a vote in which Australians had to vote for or against the Queen and the Royal Family. It was close[4]! Just over 54% voted for the Queen.

Canada has a similar system to Australia. There is also a Governor-General who does most of the Queen's duties. The Queen and the Royal family also visit regularly and have houses or palaces in Canada where they stay. Usually the Queen's visits to Canada are very popular and there is not as much discussion about the monarchy in Canada as there is in Australia. In fact many Canadians do not even know that Queen Elizabeth II is their Head of State. Most of the people in Canada who are against the monarchy live in Quebec, the French-speaking part of Canada.

And what about the other countries? Most of the countries are in the Caribbean[5] and in the Pacific Ocean[6] near Australia. Tuvalu, for example, is a group of very small islands between Australia and Hawaii. Only about 12,000 people live there and the Queen has only visited once – in 1982. Her job there is very similar to her job in Australia and Canada.

---

[1] to dissolve Parliament [dɪˈzɒlv] – *das Ende des Parlamentsjahres verkünden*, [2] Governor-General [ˌgʌvnə ˈdʒenrl] – *Generalgouverneur*, [3] to advise [ədˈvaɪz] – *(be)raten*, [4] close [kləʊs] – *knapp*, [5] Caribbean [ˌkærɪˈbiːən] – *Karibik*, [6] Pacific Ocean [pəˌsɪfɪk ˈəʊʃn] – *Pazifischer Ozean*

2 Reading

a) *Complete the diagram with the missing facts. Find a heading that fits.*

_____

	Queen
of:	▪

	Head of State		
of:	▪	▪	▪
job is done by:		▪	▪
duties/tasks	▪ ▪ ▪	▪	
at opening of Parliament	▪		
visits:		▪	▪
		▪	▪

b) *Explain what power Queen Elizabeth II has in the UK and in Australia.*

_____
_____
_____
_____
_____

c) *Compare what the Australian population feels about the Queen with what the Canadians feel about her.*

3 Writing: The Royal Family

The Royal Family is supported by money which the British people pay as taxes. Do you think they should have normal jobs like everyone else?
Answer the question. Give reasons for your opinion.

4 Modal auxiliaries

Kate Middleton knows she will probably one day be Queen of England, but she doesn't know exactly what the Queen does. She asks the Queen's private secretary some questions about her life in the last 12 months. What does she ask? What does he say?
Use to have to, to be able to, to be allowed to.

1. _____ (I, ask) questions about the Queen?

   – Yes, of course you are, Kate.

2. What does the Queen need you to do? – Well, many things, of course, but there are a lot of

   official papers which she _____ (read), and I

   _____ (bring) them to her every day in a red box.

3. Last year she was very busy. Did the Queen have any free time at all?

   – Yes, she _____ (have) time to herself in the evenings.

   And if no guests were invited, she _____ (also, have) lunch privately.

4. What about Parliament? – The Queen _____ _____ (open) and dissolve it, of course.

5. But she doesn't have any real power, does she? _____ _____ (she, change) things?

   – Well, no, she _____ (not, stop) laws.

5 Passive

Change these sentences into the passive tense.

1. They crowned the Queen of England in 1952.

   _____

2. The Queen sometimes invites famous people to lunch.

   _____

3. The Australians call the Queen 'Queen of Australia'.

   _____

4. The Queen opened a new hospital last week.

   _____

5. Since 1952 she has presented over 387,700 awards and honours.

   _____

6. The government writes 'The Speech from the Throne'.

   _____

7. The Queen has visited Canada regularly.

   _____

8. She devotes her afternoons to her social duties.

   _____

6 Mixed bag

Find the right verb and complete the sentences.

attacked · can · collecting · were demonstrating · devote · are given · joined · have · represent · was killed

People in Britain (1) _____ mixed feelings about the Queen and the Royal Family. Some people say that they (2) _____ too much money and don't really do anything. Others say that they (3) _____ Britain and are important for the country's image in the world. And the real fans (4) _____ their time to reading all about the Royal Family and (5) _____ cups and T-shirts with pictures of the Royals on them. But times (6) _____ change things fast. When Princess Diana (7) _____ in 1997, millions of people in Britain (8) _____ together to show how sad they were over her death. But in December 2010, students who (9) _____ against the government (10) _____ Prince Charles' car and broke a window.

7 The world as a good place

Complete the text.

aim · campaign · constructive · generation · hang around · member · sign up · misrepresented · join · majority

Hi, I'm Lucy, and I'm a _____ of our local youth group. But we're not just any youth group. We don't just _____ the club doing nothing. We think that the _____ of teenagers want the world to be a good place, so instead of sitting around and waiting for someone else to do something _____, we do it ourselves! We want to change how the older _____ sees us. We think we're _____ in lots of ways. A lot of people think teenagers are bored and rude and just make trouble. We _____ to show them they're wrong! So why don't you _____ us? _____ for our *Teenage Heroes*! _____ and show everyone what you're really made of!

2 Wordwise – Listening

8 Word puzzle

Read the words and find their opposites or words that are almost opposites.

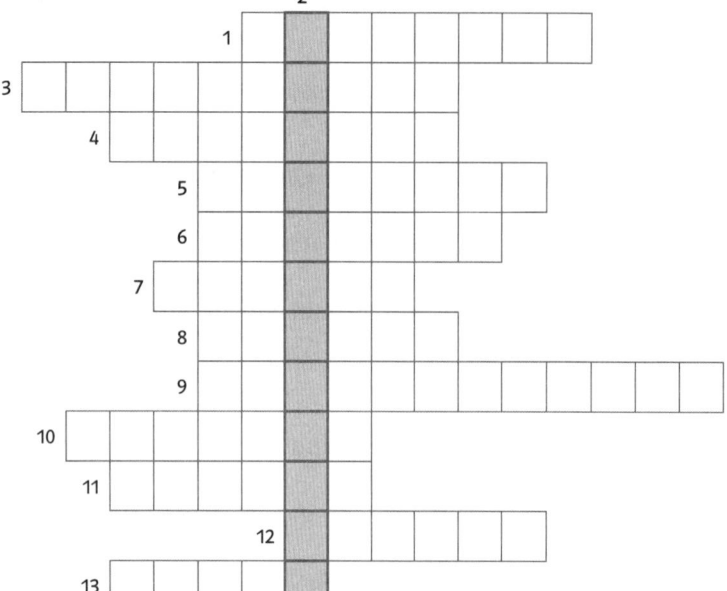

1. room
2. always
3. social
4. guilty
5. violent
6. wife
7. like
8. sunny
9. official; public
10. legal
11. unlikely
12. stop
13. every week

9 Find the word pairs

| anti- | bail | belt | chat | gas | key | make | mustard | minister | player |
| room | seat | seed | sign | social | station | tear | up | voting | prime |

1. _____ 5. _____

2. _____ 6. _____

3. _____ 7. _____

4. _____ 8. _____

9. _____ 10. _____

10 Listening: Teenage Heroes!

Lucy has organized a meeting at her local youth club. Which group is going to do which activity? Put the right letter (A–E) in the boxes. There's one picture that you don't need.

1.

2.

3.

4.

5.

6.

11 Speaking: Car-free zone

Situation: You and some of your friends are part of the *Teenage Heroes!* campaign. You have turned three streets in the town centre into a car-free zone for one day. Your job is to stop cars from driving down Water Street. You have just stopped a driver. He opens his window.

Driver: What's the matter?

You: _____ Grüße den Fahrer und frage ihn, ob es ihm etwas ausmachen würde, diese Straße heute nicht entlang zu fahren.

Driver: Why?

You: _____ Sage, dass es Teil der Teenage-Heroes!-Kampagne ist. Ihr wollt, dass die Leute öfter Fahrrad fahren, besonders im Stadtzentrum.

Driver: But you can't do that without warning! Just because you feel like it!

You: _____ Entgegne sehr höflich, dass ihr die Leute schon vorgewarnt habt. Sage, dass es seit Dienstag jeden Tag im Radio Werbung gibt.

Driver: I don't listen to the radio.

You: _____ Sage, dass dir das leid tut, aber dass es auch überall in der Nähe des Stadtzentrums Schilder gibt.

Driver: Signs?

You: _____ Bejahe und sage, dass es da drüben eines gibt. Du glaubst, dass er daran vorbeigefahren ist.

Driver: Oh ... well ... I'm sorry, I didn't see it. So, er ... who did you say you are – and why are you doing this?

You: _____ Stelle dich vor und sage, dass ihr eine Gruppe von Jugendlichen seid, die versuchen, die Stadt und die Landschaft schöner zu machen. Sage, dass ihr diese Woche viele verschiedene Aktivitäten macht.

2 Speaking – Writing – Mediation

Driver: Well, good. It's better than hanging around street corners, I suppose.
Yes, well, well done, it's nice to see teenagers doing something constructive.

You: _____ Bedanke dich.

12 Writing: Change

If could change one thing about the world, what would it be? Why?
Write about the situation now and how the situation would be if you could change it.

_____
_____
_____
_____
_____
_____
_____
_____
_____
_____

13 Mediation: Skateistan

Read the text.

Donations Needed Now to Keep Classes On

Each week 320 Afghan boys and girls come to the Skateistan NGO for skateboarding and educational classes. For many youths, this
5 is the only schooling they receive. Several of them have spent their days working on the streets of Kabul since the age of 7 or 8. And the girls have virtually no other chance to take part in sport. To keep doing what it
10 does, though, Skateistan requires donations immediately and is asking for your help.

In recent weeks thousands of people have viewed the short documentary "To Live and Skate Kabul" and discovered the Skateistan
15 project. Many people have said they'd love to help, and now is the time when it is truly needed.

At present, Skateistan requires immediate funds to support day-to-day running costs over the next few months. These costs 20
include school supplies, student meals and transport, organisation costs and housing for the international volunteer instructors. As a small organisation each dollar that is received by Skateistan is carefully spent and directly 25
contributes to the goal of giving children an alternative to poverty, drugs or fighting.

If you've watched the film and felt hopeful for Afghanistan's youth, or seen what Skateistan is doing on this website and believe the NGO is 30
achieving something positive, please think about a donation to show your support.

> Because Skateistan operates abroad through a network of international volunteers, 100% of Skateistan's budget is directed towards operations of the school in Kabul.
>
> The quickest, easiest way to donate is through PayPal, though it will take some weeks to help Skateistan in Kabul.
>
> The most effective way to help keep things running at Skateistan is to transfer money directly into Skateistan's bank account in Kabul, so that it can be used on the ground within days, perhaps buying classroom supplies or petrol to pick up the students. The account info is: …

Bearbeite die Aufgaben auf Deutsch.

1. In welcher Bedeutung wird folgender Begriff verwendet? Markiere die richtige Bedeutung.
   donation [dəʊˈneɪʃn] *Substantiv (line 1)*

   1. Dotation ☐   2. a) Spende, b) Geldspende ☐   3. Zahlung ☐

2. Deine kleine Schwester will wissen, worum es in dem Artikel geht.

   _____
   _____
   _____

3. Sie fragt, wie viele Schüler dahin gehen.

   _____
   _____

4. Sie sieht die Zahlen 7 und 8 im Text und will wissen, worauf sich diese beziehen.

   _____
   _____

5. Woher wussten die Menschen überhaupt, dass es 'Skateistan' gibt?

   _____
   _____

6. Wofür brauchen sie Geld? (3 Fakten)

   _____
   _____
   _____

7. Wie kann man Geld überweisen?

   _____
   _____
   _____

3 Listening

Topic 3 This is India!

1 Listening: On holiday in India

a) *Read the sentences. Then listen to the dialogue. A tourist couple are talking about haggling[1] over the price of a rickshaw ride in India. Tick the five correct boxes.*

The woman ...		The man ...	
1. tells the rickshaw driver where they want to go.	☐	1. asks the price of the rickshaw ride.	☐
2. says they will use another rickshaw.	☐	2. haggles with the rickshaw driver over the price.	☐
3. agrees to pay the price the driver has given.	☐	3. doesn't enjoy haggling.	☐
4. says that eight rupees is like ten pounds to them.	☐	4. offers the driver twelve rupees for the ride to the station.	☐
5. thinks the man gave the driver more than twelve rupees.	☐	5. thinks the driver enjoyed haggling over the price.	☐

b) *Find the missing words and complete the text.*

The man and the woman are going to _____,

but the driver says it will cost 20 rupees, not ten, because of

_____ . At first the man doesn't want to pay

more than _____ . The rickshaw driver

can't believe it and says that he would take the food from his

_____ . Then he says the ride would

cost _____ .

c) *Are the statements right or wrong? Tick.*

	right	wrong
1. The man thinks that the rickshaw driver tells lies[2] to get more money.		
2. The man thinks that the rickshaw driver probably has lots of children.		
3. The man thinks that tourists should pay more for rickshaw rides.		
4. He thinks that local people then couldn't afford the ride.		
5. The woman thinks it's too easy just to say "He's lying[2], so I won't give him any money."		
6. She says that she wouldn't lie, even if she was hungry.		
7. She thinks that if the driver had more money, he could buy more.		
8. She thinks that everyone would be richer.		

[1]to haggle ['hægl] – *handeln,* [2]lie/to lie [laɪ] – *Lüge; lügen*

2 Reading: The Indian fashion industry

(A) The clothes industry in India is over 7,000 years old. It all began when people in the Indus Valley in northern India started to grow cotton to make clothes. The word cotton actually comes from a Hindi word. The Indus Valley Civilisation was one of the most advanced in the world at that time. In many other areas of the world clothes were mainly[1] made from animal skins.

(B) As time passed more and more people around the world started wearing clothes made out of cotton or wool[2]. Cotton started to be grown in other countries and exported[3]. The cotton material was always made in people's houses until the industrial revolution, which started in England in the 18th century. Until that time India exported more cotton clothes and material than any other country. After that time England became the top exporter. The cotton itself though[4], still mainly came from India. It was grown there and taken to England by ship. There it was turned into material and then clothes. At one point India could not produce enough cotton for the British factories and so cotton was also bought from other countries, for example, Egypt and the USA.

(C) As Britain and other western countries became richer during and after the industrial revolution, workers in the factories began to be paid more. This meant that the cotton material and cotton clothes became more expensive. After some time it became cheaper to produce the clothes and material in India again because the people there were paid less.

(D) India is still very important in the textile industry today. Both material and clothes are produced there and exported to many other places in the world. There are different reasons for this. Firstly, India is still one of the biggest producers of cotton in the whole world. Secondly, it is very cheap to produce things in India because people there earn less. Not only are adults paid less in India but also many children still work in factories or at home. They are paid even less. Children are not allowed to work in India so they work illegally. This problem has been going on for a long time in India and many people are trying to stop it. It is difficult though. Many families in India don't have enough money to feed all their children. That's why the parents let their children work. Children who are as young as six years old work at home all day long helping to make clothes which we will later wear. Older children work in factories. Children who work like this usually die young and have no chance to go to school. It is still a big problem in India.

(E) Cotton has a long history in India, and so too does the sari. The sari was first worn thousands of years ago by the people who lived in the Indus Valley. It is still popular today. Many women wear the sari in India and in other Asian countries because it is perfect for the climate there. Nowadays[5], though, the sari is also becoming more popular in Europe and America. One reason for this is the success of Bollywood films around the world; another is that they are made out of light, colourful material, which looks beautiful in any part of the world.

[1]mainly ['meɪnli] – *hauptsächlich*, [2]wool [wʊl] – *Wolle*, [3]to export [ɪk'spɔːt] – *exportieren*, [4]though [ðəʊ] – *jedoch*, [5]nowadays ['naʊədeɪz] – *heutzutage*

a) *Match the headings with the right paragraphs.*

- Cotton goes round the world ☐
- Early beginnings of cotton ☐
- Working children ☐
- Beautiful saris ☐
- Factory production ☐

3 Reading

b) *Tick the four correct boxes.*

1. The people of the Indus valley wore animal skins. ☐
2. The word 'cotton' comes from a Hindi word. ☐
3. The industrial revolution started in 18th century India. ☐
4. Indian cotton was made into material and clothes in England. ☐
5. It was cheaper to produce cotton things in India because pay was lower. ☐
6. India does not produce much cotton now. ☐
7. The sari is a new way of wearing cotton material. ☐
8. The sari is becoming more popular in other countries. ☐

c) *Find the missing words and complete the text about working children in India.*

Cotton material and clothes can be produced cheaply in India because the

workers there _____. Although children are not _____

_____ in India, many children _____

in factories or at home. They are paid even _____.

It is difficult to stop this, although many _____. However,

if a poor family wants _____, the parents

must let the children work. Even six-year-old children work at home _____.

_____ work in factories, so they _____

to go to school and usually die young.

d) *Match the sentence parts and write the correct letters in the boxes.*

1. The sari has a long history ☐   a. because it is perfect for the climate.

2. Many women in India and other parts of Asia wear the sari ☐   b. and the style has not changed.

3. Saris are usually made of cotton ☐   c. which started in the Indus valley.

4. The sari was first worn thousands of years ago ☐   d. because of the success of Bollywood films.

5. Saris are very colourful ☐   e. though you can see beautiful silk saris, too.

6. The sari is becoming better known ☐   f. and are also comfortable to wear.

3 Reporting

Read these four short dialogues. Then write down what the day manager of a hotel in Mumbai told the night manager.

1.
Man: Hi. Can you tell me how to book a safari, please? I want to see elephants and tigers.
Manager: Yes, sure. You are Mr Peters in Room 12, aren't you? Do you want to go tomorrow? You must leave at 5 am. Is that OK?
Man: That's great, thanks. Can you call me at 4 am please?

2.
Doctor: I'm sorry, Mrs Farr in Room 121 is very ill. She must go to hospital as soon as possible.
Manager: I'll call for an ambulance.
Doctor: Mr Farr will go with her, but he will come back tonight, so keep his room for him.
Manager: Yes, of course.

3.
Woman: Hi! Can I have a room for three nights, please?
Manager: I'm sorry, I can only let you have a room for two nights. After that the hotel is full.
Woman: Oh, well, I'll take a room anyway.
Manager: Very well. That is room 116.
Woman: Thanks. I have to go out now, and I won't be back until late. Can you put my bags in the room, please?

4.
Manager: Can I help you?
Man: I want to buy a sari for my wife. Can you tell me where I can buy a nice sari that is not too expensive?
Manager: Yes, sir. My cousin has a sari shop with beautiful saris in cotton and silk. It is just down the road. It is called "Maharani Saris".
Man: Thanks!
Manager: Tell him that I sent you!

Day manager: Mr Peters in Room 12 asked me _____.

He said that _____.

So I have booked one for him tomorrow. He must leave at 5 am so he asked us _____

_____ at 4 am.

Then the doctor came to see Mrs Farr in Room 121. He said that _____

and that _____. I called an ambulance. The doctor

said that Mr Farr _____, but that _____

_____. He hasn't come back yet, so she must be very ill.

A woman wanted a room for three nights but I told her _____

_____. She said she _____

_____ anyway and I gave her room 116. She said she _____ and

_____, so I have put her bags in her room.

The man from Room 105 asked me where _____.

He wanted one that _____. I told him _____

_____ down the road called 'Maharani Saris'.

3 Listening

4 Listening: Indian dance

Listen to radio interviewer Jane Ashton talking to Mani Jaffri who has organized a big dance festival.

a) *Tick the correct box to complete the sentence.*

1. The topic of the programme is …
   A: American Indians. ☐
   B: India. ☐
   C: Indian dance. ☐

2. The dance show will be …
   A: at the O2 arena. ☐
   B: at the Festival Hall. ☐
   C: in Europe. ☐

3. There will be an extra show …
   A: every day at 2:30 pm. ☐
   B: on Saturday evening. ☐
   C: with extra entertainment. ☐

4. The dancers wear …
   A: traditional Indian costumes. ☐
   B: the latest Indian fashion. ☐
   C: modern Western clothes. ☐

5. All the dancers …
   A: come from Eastern India. ☐
   B: are acrobats, too. ☐
   C: are carrying drums. ☐

6. The men's dances …
   A: started as war dances. ☐
   B: are from different Indian traditions. ☐
   C: all have religious origins. ☐

7. The show includes …
   A: dancing and singing. ☐
   B: dancing and acting. ☐
   C: dancing, singing and acting. ☐

b) *Write down the similarities and the differences between this traditional kind of dance and Bollywood dancing?*

_____
_____
_____
_____
_____
_____

5 Odd one out

Draw a line through the word that does not fit with the others.

1. sari • kurta • cotton • shirt
2. necklace • sari • bracelet • ring
3. marble • fur • stone • wood
4. textiles • currency • engineering • hotels
5. vegetarian • belief • religious • prayer
6. settler • emperor • soldier • superpower

6 Opposites

Write the opposites of these words.

1. sunset – _____
2. high – _____
3. complicated – _____
4. enemy – _____

7 How do you say it?

Where does the stress go? Write the words in the correct box.

backpacker   compartment   complicated   currency   economy   emperor
independence   engineering   religious   selection   vegetarian

●••/●•••	•●••/•●••	••●•/••●••

8 India after 1947

Put in the correct words to complete the sentences.

India got its _____ in 1947 after a long _____. This was lead by Mahatma Gandhi (the title means 'great _____'). He tried to make sure that protests against British rule[1] were _____ because he disliked _____. Millions of Indian _____ fought on the side of Britain and her _____ in the First and Second World Wars. However, many people thought it was too soon and pointed out[2] the _____ differences in the country. Even though[3] a huge _____ became Pakistan, many people were killed in the _____ between the two countries.

[1]rule [ruːl] – *Herrschaft*, [2]to point out [pɔɪntˈaʊt] – *betonen*, [3]even though [ˈiːvn ˈðəʊ] – *obwohl*

3 Writing

9 Writing: Children in India

Look at the lines 41–66 of Ex. 2 'Reading: The Indian fashion industry' again and then read the following facts.

Children at work in India

Children under 14 are not allowed to do dangerous work in factories or mines.	Girls are often seen as 'helpers' not 'workers' so they are not protected by the law.
Children work in the home for outside pay. They do small, boring tasks over and over again.	Children work on large farms, sometimes working long hours doing hard physical work.

Now write a short report on children's work in India. Write about 120 words. Remember to include facts, not your opinions. Think about:
- why families want their children to work;
- why the Indian economy profits from children working;
- what it does to the children.

_____
_____
_____
_____
_____
_____
_____
_____

10 Writing: Making a protest

Write an e-mail or a letter to a newspaper about children working in India and suggest what people in your country could do to help these children. Write about 120 words.

_____
_____
_____
_____
_____
_____
_____
_____

11 Speaking: About India

You will need two different partners, one for part a) and a different partner for part b).

a) *Write down five things you would like to see and do in India. Say why you want to go there.*

I would like to:	because:
1.	
2.	
3.	
4.	
5.	

Now talk to a partner. Tell your partner in <u>two minutes</u> what you want to see or do, and find out in another <u>two minutes</u> what your partner would like to see or do in India. Take short notes.

_____ would like to:	because:
1.	
2.	
3.	
4.	
5.	

b) *Use your notes to tell a second partner in <u>one minute</u> some of the things that your first partner said.*

12 Mediation: Indian fashion

Situation: Deine Mutter interessiert sich für einen Artikel über indische Mode in einer englischen Modezeitschrift, aber sie versteht nicht alles. Beantworte ihre Fragen auf Deutsch.

Bollywood film stars often wear dresses made from sari material with beautiful gold edges.

Mother: Das ist wohl eine indische Filmschauspielerin, aber was steht da über das Kleid?

You: _____

Mother: Das ist aber kein Sari! Was steht da dazu?

You: _____

Fashion dresses have their origins in saris, but are made differently.

Both men and women can feel comfortable in hot weather when they wear a kurta. It's a simple cotton shirt, loose and easy to wear and it comes in bright colours and patterns. In plain, fresh white it looks really cool.

Mother: Shirt kenne ich, aber was ist das mit den Farben?

You: _____

Topic 4 Choices and decisions

1 Listening: Talking about the future

a) *Listen to the dialogue. Are the statements right or wrong? Tick.*

	right	wrong
1. William is going to stay on at school next year.		
2. Anneena wouldn't like to work for William's dad.		
3. William's brother and sister don't work for their dad.		
4. If William's dad had to sell his company, he would be very sad.		
5. The company produces steel.		
6. William's dad finished school at the age of 15.		

b) *Match the sentence parts. Write the correct letters in the boxes.*

1. William is going to try working for his dad ☐
2. His parents think he's not old enough ☐
3. Anneena thinks it would be better ☐
4. Working and then going to college later ☐
5. William would get the firm ☐

a. to decide for himself.
b. can be really difficult.
c. and then leave if he doesn't like it.
d. when his dad gets too old.
e. if he got some qualifications.

c) *Tick the correct box.*

1. Anneena thinks that working for her dad would be …
   A: great. ☐
   B: difficult. ☐
   C: easy. ☐

2. William has got …
   A: an older brother and sister. ☐
   B: no brothers and sisters. ☐
   C: a younger brother and sister. ☐

3. William would like to …
   A: go to Sixth Form College. ☐
   B: earn some money. ☐
   C: go to Art College. ☐

4. William's brother went to Africa …
   A: before he went to university. ☐
   B: after he finished university. ☐
   C: before he finished university. ☐

5. Aneena is going to be a doctor because …
   A: it's what she always wanted to do. ☐
   B: it's a tradition in her family. ☐
   C: her father told her to. ☐

6. Anneena would also like to …
   A: study[1] football. ☐
   B: study sport and play football. ☐
   C: become a sports reporter. ☐

[1]to study ['stʌdi] – *studieren, lernen*

4 Reading

2 Reading: Salford College

Are you leaving school?
We offer a range[1] of courses at different levels to prepare you for your career. Our courses build on each other so you can choose the right level and continue until you get the qualification which you need whether you want to go to university or get a job.

What do you need to do?
First you need to choose which career you would like to go into and then choose the right level. When you have decided on the course you would like, you need to apply for it.

How do you apply?
First you need to fill in our application form. You can get this from the college or download it from our website. You need to send it to us before the 30th April. If you have any questions about the form or need help to fill it in, you can contact our office. When we have received your application, we will invite you for an interview.

Choose a course
Before you choose your course, you need to decide on your career. It is often a good idea to try different internships and to talk to people who work in that career. If you are not sure, you can choose an introduction course to find out whether it is the right subject for you. Below is a list of subjects and courses in alphabetical order.

Animal Care
Art and Design
Building
Business Studies

In **Business Studies** you learn about the different areas in the real world of business. There are courses in human resources, marketing, sales, finance and public relations. Students learn to develop the practical and personal skills which they will need for their career in business. During the course students can concentrate on the sector of industry which they are most interested in.
You can choose from three courses:

Level 1:	Students should be interested in business and be good at Maths and English. Qualifications in IT can be done at the same time. After completing this course, students can take the course leading to the first diploma.
Level 2 (Diploma in Business):	Students should have 4 GCSEs with at least grade D. There are no exams in the course; you will be marked[2] on coursework. During this course you will need to do a placement in a business of your choice. After the course you can start your career in the world of business or go on to do the Advanced Diploma in Business.
Level 3 (Advanced Diploma in Business):	Students should have at least 4 GCSEs with grades A–C. The course will concentrate on finance, communication, IT skills and personal skills and will include a placement in a business of your choice. After the course you can start your career in the world of business or start a university course.

[1]range [reindʒ] – *Auswahl*, [2]to mark [mɑːk] – *hier: benoten*

a) *Find out from the text what order you must do things in and write a checklist.*

1. Try _____
   or choose _____
2. Decide _____
3. _____
4. _____
5. _____
6. _____
7. Wait to be _____

b) *You have applied to do the course in business studies. To prepare for the interview look at the information about this course and write <u>notes</u> on*
- *what you find interesting about this course,*
- *why you want to do the course,*
- *why this is the right course for you.*

3 Writing: An application

Look at the text about Salford College again. As part of the application form you must write a short text saying why you want to study that course at Salford. Use the notes you made in exercise 2 b) and write about 120 words.

4 Language

4 What people should do

Read about the situation and the options. Then say what you think the people should or shouldn't do.

1. Jessie is 15. She had a boyfriend but he has left her and she is three months pregnant[1].
   Jessie could:
   - not tell anyone yet
   - tell her parents
   - tell all her friends at school
   - tell a teacher
   - see a doctor
   - tell her ex-boyfriend or her ex-boyfriend's parents
   - go to an advice centre for teenage mums

   I think she _____

   _____

   _____

   _____

   _____

   [1] pregnant ['pregnənt] – *schwanger*

2. Matt is 15. He stole some money from his mother and he took a neighbour's motorcycle. He crashed the bike. He thought the bike was a wreck so he ran home. Nobody saw him.
   Matt could:
   - tell his parents about the money and the motorcycle
   - tell his neighbour about the motorcycle
   - tell the police
   - do nothing and say that he was in his room at the time
   - tell all his friends but not his parents or the neighbour

   I think he _____

   _____

   _____

   _____

   _____

3. Don, 16, copied the answers from his friend in an important exam. He was surprised when he got better marks than his friend.
   Don could:
   - talk to his friend about it
   - tell a teacher
   - tell his parents
   - do nothing

   I think Don _____

   _____

   _____

   _____

5 Writing: Giving advice

Choose two of the following letters and answer them. What advice would you give to the people?

(1) Dear Agony Angel,

I'm a 15-year-old boy and in Year 11 at school. I'm taking my GCSEs next year and I cannot cope with¹ the pressure from my school and my parents. I can't sleep at night because I worry about my grades, and I don't go out any more because I don't have the time. I can't go on! Please help me! Yours, Robert

(2) Hi there,

I'm afraid my friend has a drinking problem and I'm fed up with always hanging out in pubs and ending up drunk. Every time he drinks, I feel I have to drink, too, because I can cope so much better when I'm a little drunk myself. I don't know what to do. Molly (16)

(3) Dear Christopher,

I have a very personal problem: I'm two-and-a-half months pregnant². I'm sixteen years old and I go to comprehensive school. My parents will kill me. What should I do? I'm desperate, please help me! Love, Cathy

(4) Dear Agony Angel Christopher,

I'm fed up with my mum and dad. I've got a disabled³ brother and he gets more attention⁴ than I do. If my brother does anything wrong, they never seem to say very much but if I do anything wrong, I always get into trouble. Sometimes I feel really angry. Ben (14)

¹to cope with ['kəʊp wɪð] – *umgehen mit*, ²pregnant ['pregnənt] – *schwanger*, ³disabled [dɪ'seɪbld] – *behindert*, ⁴attention [ə'tenʃn] – *Aufmerksamkeit*

4 Listening – Wordwise

6 Listening: Where are they?

Listen to these five short dialogues. Which pictures match the dialogues? Write the number of the dialogue in the box.

A ☐   B ☐   C ☐

D ☐   E ☐   F ☐

There's no dialogue for one picture: Which one? _____

7 Word box: In hospital

Look at the definitions and find the right words.

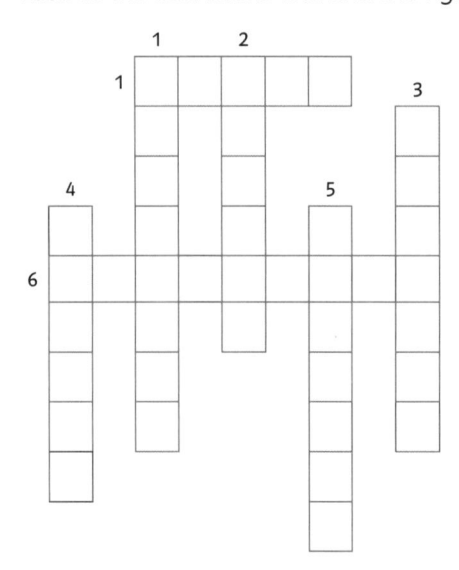

Across: →
1. take sb into hospital
6. You might have to have this in hospital.

Down: ↓
1. … nervosa
2. of the mind (*Kopf, Geist*)
3. It makes you sick.
4. sb who tries to help sick people
5. sth that makes you ill

8 Which word?

Complete the sentences with the correct word.

1. Tom wants to work on a farm, but first he's going to go to college to learn about

   _____ .

2. His brother James is already doing _____ at college. He's doing a course in

   _____ because he wants to design gardens.

3. One of the students on James's course can't walk. She's in a _____ because

   she had an accident four years ago. She has had several _____ and spent a lot

   of time in _____ .

4. James and Tom think they're lucky. They've never had a serious _____ . When

   they finish their courses, they believe they will find _____ quickly,

   although they _____ the difficulties of finding a job.

5. James also sees _____ as an option if he could

   _____ to find enough people who would let him design their gardens. But he

   understands the _____ of finding customers.

9 Writing: Advice to a friend

Your friends send you texts. Text them back with some advice.

1. Hi! Have you got Alicia's new phone number? She said she's not speaking to me but I know she doesn't really mean it. Now she has a new phone. Can you help? Terry

   _____

   _____

2. Help! Am in town, no money for bus or food. Can you help? Odd man looking at me all the time. Marie

   _____

   _____

3. Hi! Pat and I want to go to the Underground (club) tonight. Can you come too and bring a friend? Might be late so miss school tomorrow! Jinx

   _____

   _____

4 Speaking – Mediation

10 Speaking: Non-electronic-media week

Your friend's mum has read about a 'non-electronic-media' week and wants to try it out in her family. Talk about it for two minutes – you can be for or against it. Read the facts first.

For one week nobody in the family will	The family members are allowed to
• watch TV, • listen to the radio • use the Internet (no e-mails!) • use a mobile in any way • use an MP3 player or walkman	• use the computer to write texts, letters • read books, newspapers and magazines • play an instrument, sing • do any hobby that does not need electronic devices

List your reasons for or against the idea.

_____
_____
_____
_____
_____

11 Mediation: How school can help

Situation: Your cousin Brad in the US wants to know what German schools do about bullies. You find this article about a big school in Hessen where they have a social worker with two assistants to help pupils.

Read about how they help and their project week. Answer Brad's questions with information from this website or from your own school.

DIE SOZIALARBEIT AN DER RICARDA-HUCH-SCHULE

Unsere Sozialarbeiterin stellt die Bedürfnisse von Schülerinnen und Schülern in den Mittelpunkt ihrer Arbeit. Mit ihren zwei Assistent/-innen will sie die Lebens- und Lernverhältnisse der Schülerinnen und Schüler verbessern.

1. Die Sozialarbeiterin und ihre Beratungshelfer/-innen können individuell beraten. Sie sind Ansprechpartner für Schüler, Lehrer und Eltern. Das kann in Einzelgesprächen oder in Gruppen geschehen. Sie versuchen, in vertraulicher Atmosphäre die Problemsituation zu klären. Andere Beratungsstellen, z. B. Suchthilfe, können hinzugezogen werden.

2. Die Sozialarbeiterin und ihre Helfer bieten Freizeitaktivitäten zur Entspannung an. Das kann alles von Sport über Theater und Handarbeit bis hin zu besonderen Gesprächs- runden sein.

GEWALTPRÄVENTION

1. In der 8. Klasse findet eine **Projektwoche zum Thema „Gewalt – Soziales Lernen"** statt. In der Projektwoche
   - wird das Thema der Gewalt ausführlich behandelt,
   - wird eine Definition von Gewalt zusammen erarbeitet,
   - setzen sich die Schülerinnen und Schüler mit ihren eigenen Aggressionen auseinander.

2. Für alle Schülerinnen und Schüler steht ein **„Kummerkasten"** zur Verfügung. Durch Einwerfen eines Zettels können sie um Hilfe bei persönlichen Problemen oder bei Problemsituationen mit Freunden oder in der Klassengemeinschaft bitten. Die Sozialhelfer/-innen versuchen durch Einzelgespräche und Gesprächsrunden Situationen zu klären und die Probleme zu lösen.

Brad: You said you'd got some information about how schools stop bullies. Can you tell me about it?

You: Well, I can tell you what they do at the Ricarda-Huch-Schule. They have _____ _____ and they try to _____

Brad: How do they do that? Who can they talk to?

You: They _____

Brad: Are these all one-to-one conversations?

You: No, _____

Brad: Do they do anything else?

You: Yes, _____

And in year 8 _____

Brad: That sounds great. But how do the students get help with problems?

You: The school has a special box: _____

_____

_____

The social workers try to deal with[1] the situation _____

_____

Übersicht über die Aufgabentypen

Topic	Aufgabe	Aufgabentyp	offen	halboffen	geschlossen	Schwerpunkte
1	1a)–d)	Hörverstehen Detailverständnis			✓	Inhalt eines Gesprächs verstehen
	2a)–c)	Leseverstehen Detailverständnis			✓	Inhalt eines Sachtextes erfassen
	2d)	Leseverstehen Globalverständnis			✓	
	3	Grammatik			✓	Revision: present and past tenses
	4	Grammatik			✓	Relative pronouns
	5	Grammatik			✓	Comparison of adjectives
	6	Sprechen/ Schreiben		✓		ein telefonisches Bewerbungsgespräch führen
	7	Schreiben	✓			Informationen über sich selbst in ein Bewerbungsformular schreiben
	8	Hör-/Sehverstehen Globalverständnis			✓	Inhalt eines Gesprächs verstehen und dementsprechend Bilder einander zuordnen
	9	Lexik			✓	Wortschatz des Topic: Crossword
	10	Lexik			✓	Wortschatz des Topic: Opposites
	11	Lexik			✓	Wortschatz des Topic: Word families
	12	Schreiben	✓			die eigene Meinung wiedergeben
	13	Mediation		✓		wesentliche Informationen in der Muttersprache wiedergeben

Topic	Aufgabe	Aufgabentyp	offen	halboffen	geschlossen	Schwerpunkte
2	1a), b)	Hörverstehen Detailverständnis			✓	Inhalt eines Gesprächs verstehen
	1c)	Hörverstehen Globalverständnis			✓	
	2a)	Leseverstehen Detailverständnis			✓	Inhalt eines Sachtextes erfassen
	2b), c)	Leseverstehen/ Schreiben Detailverständnis		✓		Aspekte eines Sachtextes zusammenfassen
	3	Schreiben	✓			die eigene Meinung zum Thema Royal Family wiedergeben
	4	Grammatik			✓	Modal auxiliaries
	5	Grammatik/ Schreiben			✓	Passive
	6	Grammatik			✓	Mixed bag
	7	Lexik			✓	Wortschatz des Topic
	8	Lexik			✓	Wortschatz des Topic: Word puzzle
	9	Lexik			✓	Wortschatz des Topic: Word pairs
	10	Hör-/Sehverstehen Globalverständnis			✓	Inhalt eines Gesprächs verstehen und ihn Bildern zuordnen
	11	Sprechen/ Schreiben		✓		den Sinn eines Umweltprojekts erläutern
	12	Schreiben	✓			die eigene Meinung wiedergeben
	13	Mediation		✓		wesentliche Informationen in der Muttersprache wiedergeben

Übersicht Aufgabentypen · A

Topic	Aufgabe	Aufgabentyp	offen	halboffen	geschlossen	Schwerpunkte
3	1a)–c)	Hörverstehen Detailverständnis			✓	Inhalt eines Gesprächs verstehen
	2a)	Leseverstehen Globalverständnis			✓	Inhalt eines Sachtextes erfassen
	2b)–d)	Leseverstehen Detailverständnis			✓	
	3	Grammatik			✓	*Reported speech*
	4	Hörverstehen Detailverständnis			✓	Inhalt eines Gesprächs verstehen
	5	Lexik			✓	Wortschatz des *Topic: Odd one out*
	6	Lexik			✓	Wortschatz des *Topic: Opposites*
	7	Lexik			✓	Wortschatz des *Topic: Word stress*
	8	Lexik			✓	Wortschatz des *Topic*
	9	Schreiben		✓		einen Bericht über Kinderarbeit in Indien schreiben
	10	Schreiben	✓			eine formelle E-Mail bzw. einen Leserbrief schreiben
	11	Sprechen	✓			mit einem Partner/einer Partnerin über Indien sprechen
	12	Mediation		✓		wesentliche Informationen in der Muttersprache wiedergeben

Topic	Aufgabe	Aufgabentyp	offen	halboffen	geschlossen	Schwerpunkte
4	1a)–c)	Hörverstehen Detailverständnis			✓	Inhalt eines Gesprächs verstehen
	2a)	Leseverstehen Detailverständnis			✓	Inhalt eines Sachtextes erfassen
	2b)	Leseverstehen/ Schreiben Detailverständnis		✓		
	3	Schreiben	✓			eine Begründung für eine Bewerbung schreiben
	4	Grammatik/ Schreiben		✓		*Giving advice: should/shouldn't*
	5	Schreiben	✓			jemanden bei einem persönlichen Problem beraten
	6	Hör-/Sehverstehen Globalverständnis			✓	Inhalte kurzer Gespräche verstehen und ihnen Bilder zuordnen
	7	Lexik			✓	Wortschatz des *Topic: In hospital*
	8	Lexik			✓	Wortschatz des *Topic*
	9	Schreiben		✓		jemanden bei einem persönlichen Problem beraten
	10	Sprechen		✓		mit Hilfe von Stichworten und Notizen zusammenhängend und strukturiert sprechen
	11	Mediation		✓		wesentliche Informationen in der Fremdsprache wiedergeben

Lösungen

Topic 1

1 Listening: Skype

Text:

Sven: Hello? Merve? Hello? Can you hear me?
Merve: Yes, I can hear and see you. Wow, this is great. I've never used Skype before. Hello. Can you hear me?
Sven: Yes. Hi, Merve. But I can't see you. Have you plugged your camera in?
Merve: Oh no. I forgot. Wait a minute! Hi, can you see me now?
Sven: Yes. It's nice to meet you at last, Merve.
Merve: Yes, it's nice to see you, too, but actually, I'm called Merve.
Sven: Oh, I'm sorry. Merve. Is that right?
Merve: Yes, more or less. It's funny, isn't it? Just getting to know somebody on the Internet! I've never done that before.
Sven: Oh, I have. Quite a lot really. A couple of years ago we lived in the north of Sweden where not many other people live at all, so it was really good to be able to talk to other people around Sweden and around the world. I used to spend hours on the Internet every day, because there wasn't much else to do.
Merve: Oh, what were you doing in the north of Sweden?
Sven: Well, my parents wanted to take some time out from life in Stockholm, so they bought a big house and turned it into a hotel.
Merve: Oh, that's interesting. Do lots of people go on holiday in the north of Sweden then?
Sven: Yes, lots of people go from all over the world. People go there in the winter to go cross-country skiing and in the summer people enjoy hiking and fishing.
Merve: Really? Is that why your English is so good then?
Sven: Well, it's one reason, but you know in Sweden you learn English at school and almost all films are shown in English, too, so you get used to it.
Merve: Oh, I wish they showed the films in English here in Germany, too. It's so annoying; most of the films in our cinemas or on TV are made in English but you never get the chance to watch them in English. How crazy is that!
Sven: So, how did you learn to speak English so fluently?
Merve: My dad's a basketball coach. In fact he used to play basketball professionally so we lived in the States for a year. And that's where I got interested in mangas.
Sven: Ah! Is that where you learnt all your amazing techniques?
Merve: No, I was only 10 when I lived in the States, but that's where I started drawing. And how did you learn how to animate your characters so well?
Sven: Well, when we lived in the north of Sweden, there was nothing to do and, as I said, I spent a lot of time on the computer so I used to download characters and animate them to make my little sister laugh.
Merve: That's nice. And do you think you could help me with some animés if I send you my drawings?
Sven: Yes, I'd love to.
Merve: Oh, the Internet is great, isn't it? You can do anything on it, even meet people from almost anywhere in the whole world.
Sven: Yes, it's great, but really I think I'd prefer just to meet you in a café around the corner.
Merve: Yes, that would be nice.

a) 1. wrong; 2. right; 3. wrong; 4. wrong; 5. wrong; 6. wrong; 7. right; 8. wrong; 9. right; 10. right
b) 1. He spent hours on the Internet.
   2. They lived in Stockholm.
   3. They bought a big house and turned it into a hotel.
c) holiday, winter, enjoy, shown
d) ✓ using Skype
   ✓ films in English
   ✓ Sven's animés
   ✓ Sven making his sister laugh
   ✓ the Internet

2 Reading: About the English language

a) areas: in many parts of the world, in many areas of life;
reasons why lingua franca: Britain played important role in the world, the USA;
influenced by languages like: Norse, French, Latin, German, Hindi, Gaelic, Haitian, Greek;
influenced by historical events like: Norman Conquest, World Wars I and II;
influenced by famous people like: Shakespeare, William the Conqueror;

number of new words every year: 25,000; reasons for that: from other languages, inventions; grammar: is changing, too

b) 5th century: ship, that, bath
9th century: Vikings attacked England, brought own language; sky, leg
11th and 12th centuries: England attacked by Normans, William the Conqueror – king, French words entered the language; prison, prince, flower
time of Shakespeare: made up lots of new words, old words for new things; lonely, hurry, excellent

c) Many different events in history have added new words to the English language. Some words come from other countries which attacked England or through wars like World Wars I and II. A lot of modern English words come from the US, where many new things were invented, like the computer or the laptop.

d) 2.

3 Revision: Past or present?

1. have been speaking;   2. brought;
3. developed, uses;   4. had attacked;   5. began;
6. hadn't even existed;   7. has come, have entered;   8. are still changing

4 *who, which* or *whose*?

which, who, whose, which, which, which, who, whose

5 Comparatives and superlatives

most amazed, more obvious, most important, more important, most common, best, more fluently, hottest, most arrogant

6 Speaking: A phone call for a job

You: Hello, my name is (*your name*). I saw your ad in the newspaper today and I'd like to apply for a job with your firm/company.
You: Yes, IT is my favourite subject at school.
You: Yes, but my final exams are next month.
You: I come from (*your town/city*) in Germany and I'd like to work abroad, particularly in the UK.
You: I'm sorry, could you say that again, please?
You: No, I can't speak English very well. Er, what I meant to say was, I can speak English, but sometimes I make mistakes.
You: I like working in a team and I'd be interested in being an office junior.
You: Thank you very much for your time.

7 Writing: Application form

Lösungsvorschlag:
Name: Max Mustermann
Address: Hauptstraße 1, 01234 Musterstadt, Germany
Telephone: +49 (0)123/456778
E-mail: m.mustermann@internet.de
Nationality: German
Education: secondary school (name and address of your school)
Work experience: holiday job and part-time job at computer shop
Job at the moment: school, weekend job at computer shop
Position you are applying for: office junior
Special skills: IT, media design, languages (English, French)
Personality: polite, helpful, responsible
Good things about you: good at listening, don't panic easily
Things you could improve: sometimes shy, afraid of spiders
Family: father: IT teacher, mother: music teacher, two brothers
Goal(s): to design special software that is sold internationally
One more thing …: I am a very good friend, friends are important to me

8 Listening: English speakers from around the world

Text:

Sebastian: Well, hi everyone and welcome to our Animé Summer Camp here in Frankfurt. My name's Sebastian and I'm really excited that you're all here, and that you've come from all over the world. And because this is an international summer camp, all sessions and presentations will be in English, of course. OK, but before we start our work groups, everyone should introduce themselves. Please tell us your name and perhaps a little bit about yourself, and then – to make it a bit more interesting – describe your country's flag. But don't tell us which country it is – we have to guess that part!
So … who wants to … OK, the girl at the back with short, blonde hair?

Marisha: Hi, my name's Marisha, I started doing animé two years ago, and I'm really excited to be here … er … and a little nervous … and … er … oh, yeah, my flag is two green triangles, one at the top and one at the bottom, two black triangles at the sides and a yellow cross. And I'm glad the camp is in English because we all speak English where I come from!

Sebastian: Thanks, Marisha. So, who's next? Right, the guy over there with long, black hair and the red T-shirt?

Kojo: My name is Kojo and I come from … oops, almost said it! Well, where I come from we have our own language but English is the official language too. So I am happy I don't have to speak German. And my flag is nice … I like it … it has three stripes, red, yellow and green – the red one is at the top – and there is a black star in the middle.

Sebastian: Great! And – yes, you, please, with the green shirt.

David: Hi everyone, I'm David and it's great to be here with you all. And I've already seen some familiar faces from last year's camp, so I already feel at home. Anyway some of you already know where I'm from, but for those of you who don't, my flag is red with sort of a flower in the middle.

Sebastian: Thanks, David. OK, yes, what about you next – hey, cool trousers!

Samiya: Thanks! Well, hi, I'm Samiya, and I'm still at school, but I want to be an artist when I leave, so … yeah, I thought it would be a great experience to go to an animé summer camp. I've done a lot of mangas and done my own storyboards, but I haven't done much animé yet, so I hope I'll learn a lot this week. OK, and my flag has three stripes, orange, white and green and it has a sort of circle in the middle. It's not just a circle – it's called the Ashoka Chakra, but … well …

Sebastian: Thanks, Samiya. OK, ahm … there are so many of you, that it would take too long for everyone to say something, so let's just have one more person – maybe you, over there, with the long, blonde hair and the beard …

Zak: Hi, I'm Zak. Well, ahm … I've been doing animé for about five years, and … ah … well, I'm a real screenager, I guess. I spend at least six hours a day in front of the screen, but animé is my passion and I wouldn't want to do anything else. So, that's it, really.

Sebastian: Well you've come to the right place, Zak! But could you just tell us about your flag?

Zak: Oh, yeah. Well, I guess you all know it – it's red and white with a maple leaf on it.

Sebastian: Oh, yeah, I guess we've all seen that one! Well, thanks everybody, and now let's guess where they all come from. What about Marisha …?

2E (Canada);   3A (India);   4F (Ghana);
5C (Hong Kong);   6B (Jamaica)

9 Synonyms and definitions

Down: 1. nationality;   2. bilingual;
3. interviewer;   6. vegetarian;   10. trial
Across: 4. participant;   5. include;
7. goods;   8. trader;   9. fluent;
11. amazed;   12. rapid

10 Find the opposites

include ≠ leave out;   shower ≠ bath;
immediately ≠ later;   non-official ≠ official;
foreign language ≠ mother tongue;
future ≠ past;   final ≠ first;   unlike ≠ like

11 Word families

emigrated, immersion, fluent, majority, mixture, passion, professional, talented, hopeless

12 Writing: Your opinion

1. *Lösungsvorschlag:*
I think that in the year 2050 English will still be the most commonly spoken and written language. China is becoming more and more important and may soon be the country with the most influence in the world. In 2050 there will be more Chinese speakers than English speakers but I do not believe that Chinese will replace English. Even today more people speak Chinese as their mother tongue than English. But Chinese is a very difficult language. English is much easier and will probably have more 'foreign' words in 2050 than it has today. I think its grammar and spelling will change, too. Maybe there won't

be so many difficult words and not so many tenses. Spanish and Hindi may become more important as populations who speak these languages are increasing rapidly. But I don't believe that there will be one global language in 2050. Maybe that will happen in the year 2500.

2. *Lösungsvorschläge:*
No, I wouldn't like to have bilingual sports lessons. German isn't my mother tongue and I have problems with lessons in German anyway. I find English very difficult and it would be like having an English lesson at the same time as a sports lesson. Then I wouldn't enjoy sports at all.
Or:
Yes, I think that would be great! Lots of sports words are English anyway, so I don't think it would be a problem. It would help my English, too. Maybe I would learn more words and it could help me with my grammar because it would be like doing sports in an English or American school.

13 Mediation: The official language in the US

1. Die USA haben nie eine offizielle Sprache gehabt. Es gab nie eine Abstimmung zu diesem Thema.
2. 1795 gab es im Kongress eine Abstimmung über die Übersetzung von Gesetzen ins Deutsche. Die Idee wurde aber ein paar Monate später aufgegeben.
3. Die Nazis haben die Legende verbreitet, um der deutschen Sprache mehr Gewicht auf der internationalen Bühne zu verleihen. Diesen Wunsch haben sie mit der Geschichte über die Abstimmung vermischt.

Zusätzlicher Text für das Hörverstehen: Phoning a hotline

Recorded message:
Hello, thank you for calling British trains. We would like to improve our service to you and so some calls are recorded and used for training purposes. If you don't wish your call to be recorded, please say so during the call.
So that we can help you more quickly, please dial one of the following numbers.
Dial 1 for information about today's train travel.
Dial 2 if you want to book a ticket to travel today.
Dial 3 if you want to book a ticket to travel in the future.
Dial 4 for international train travel
Dial 5 to speak to an operator.

   Brigitte: Five.

Recorded message:
I'm sorry all our operators are busy, please try again at some later time.

   Emma: What's the matter?
   Brigitte: They're all busy, I have to call again later.
   Emma: Oh, I don't believe it. These call centres are terrible, aren't they?
   Brigitte: Yes, It takes ten minutes before you find out that you can't speak to anybody.

Recorded message:
… Dial 5 to speak to an operator.
   Brigitte: Five.
   Operator: Yes, how can I help you?
   Brigitte: Hello. Er, I left my bag yesterday on the train and I wanted to know if anybody had found it.
   Operator: Which train were you travelling on?
   Brigitte: I was travelling on the 2:15 London Euston to Manchester Piccadilly.
   Operator: And whereabouts on the train do you think you left your bag?
   Brigitte: Oh, well, I put it on the shelf above my seat and when I came back from the wc, my bag was gone.
   Operator: I'm sorry; I didn't understand that, could you repeat it, please?
   Brigitte: Yes, I put my bag on the shelf above my seat and then I went to the VC.
   Operator: I'm sorry. Where did you go?
   Brigitte: Oh, I'm sorry, I went to the toilet and when I came back, my bag was gone.
   Operator: Oh, you mean it was stolen?
   Brigitte: Well, somebody could have taken it by mistake.
   Operator: That's not very likely, though, is it?
   Brigitte: Well, no, maybe not …
   Operator: So, I'm afraid you'll need to call the railway police. They deal with everything that has to do with crime. You'll need the phone number 08105 345 7684.
   Brigitte: Oh, I'm sorry. I didn't understand. Could you say that again, please?
   Operator: Yes, you'll need to call the railway police on 08105 345 7684.

Zusätzlicher Text für das Leseverstehen: A super summer in the middle of nowhere[1]

When I got off the bus in Bemidji, Minnesota, I thought maybe I had a made a mistake. I was going to spend my whole summer here? In this little town? There really didn't seem to be much here. But then everything changed. I got picked up and driven to the Concordia Language Villages on Turtle Lake outside of Bemidji. And if I thought there was "not much" in Bemidji, well, here there was much less of that "not much". I was in the middle of the woods with just a few buildings around. But then everything changed again. Suddenly there were people all over, lots of them my age. I overheard people speaking German and French and Spanish and … well, everything except English! It didn't take long for me to make friends with other kids who were here to be counselors[2], too.

I had wanted to do something different with my summer. I thought about working in the US, but it isn't always easy to get permission. Then I remembered learning about how popular summer camps are in America and decided to check that out. I was looking on the Internet and in a forum I found the Concordia Language Villages, which are language immersion camps, and thought it clearly sounded like something for me – spending my summer working with kids, teaching them my mother tongue (German) and showing them my culture. I tried my luck and applied for a position as a junior counselor. Imagine my happiness when I was contacted and told that they wanted me to come and work for them!

The German camp, called Waldsee (all of the language camps' names translate into Lake of the Woods), is very nice with buildings called 'Bahnhof', 'Gasthaus' (where they serve only German-style food) and 'Schwarzwaldhaus'. It almost looks like home – just a bit exaggerated. When I got there, we had just three days of coaching to get ready before the campers arrived for the first camp session. The first task was choosing a German name. Of course I didn't have to because I'm already German, but the other counselors changed from John to Jonas or Jennifer was replaced by Renate. Then we talked about the different projects. The kids shouldn't just learn the language in a classroom setting, they should learn the language, lifestyle and culture through activities. For example, the German camp offers soccer, a sport called 'Völkerball', painting, baking, singing and theater among all the common camp activities like boating, swimming and biking are also in German.

Counselor responsibilities also include more serious things like planning, teamwork, being a leader and solving problems. The more experienced[3] counselors (many are former campers) shared their tips on how to deal with a homesick camper, make the campers into a real team and assess difficult situations. I felt well prepared for my two weeks with the campers. Even if Waldsee is really in the middle of nowhere, I didn't even notice it because I was so busy organizing activities, laughing, teaching, drying[4] tears and having a great time. I think both the campers and the counselors influence each other, learn a lot and grow up a lot in just two weeks. Certainly nobody was fluent but the shy campers who could only just say "hallo" when they arrived, managed a loud "Tschüss, bis nächstes Jahr" when they left. I definitely improved my communication skills. This camp was a great experience!

Concordia Language Villages
- started 1961
- camp languages: Arabic, Chinese, Danish, English, Finnish, French, German, Italian, Japanese, Norwegian, Portuguese, Russian, Spanish, Swedish
- minimum age for junior counselors: 16
- pay: $175 for two weeks plus meals and a room

[1]nowhere – *nirgendwo*, [2]counselor – *Betreuer/-in*, [3]experienced – *erfahren*, [4]to dry – *trocknen*

Topic 2

1 Listening: Changing the world

Text:

Emma: Oh, have you seen that? Another teenager has been killed not far away from here.
James: Oh no. That's terrible. It makes you scared, doesn't it?
Emma: It doesn't make me scared. It's only kids in gangs who get killed, isn't it?
James: No, that's not true. Quite a few totally innocent teenagers have been killed over the last few years.
Emma: Have they? How do you know?
James: Well, I'm in a political youth group and we talk about things like that and sometimes we go to council meetings so we find out what's happening.
Emma: Do you? Isn't that totally boring?
James: No, it's really interesting. We find out lots and we talk about how we could improve things and sometimes we work on campaigns.
Emma: Do you? So, who are in these gangs?
James: There are some school gangs around here who are violent. You must have read about them.
Emma: I have, but I don't always believe what I read in the paper. I thought that's typical – they always say young people are responsible for everything that goes wrong.
James: Yes, well, they're right sometimes. Teenage gangs have killed five non-gang teenagers in the last few years.
Emma: That's terrible. I'm shocked. Now I can understand why my grandad says that teenagers who have got nothing better to do should have to go in the army for a year or two.
James: Oh, Emma. Why should that help?
Emma: Well, my grandad says people learn things in the army and it would stop them hanging around street corners.
James: Oh, that's rubbish. Why should learning to kill people stop teenagers being in gangs or hanging around street corners? When I'm Prime Minister, I'll make sure we spend less on the army and more on education. That's the only way to make our society a better place.
Emma: You don't really want to become a politician, do you James?
James: Yes, I do. Why shouldn't I?
Emma: Oh, politics is so boring. And you'd have to sit and listen to people all day long, talking about money and laws and everybody knows politicians can't change things anyway. Not really. They all talk a lot about what they are going to do when they win the election, then they win and do the opposite.
James: That isn't true. OK. Obviously it happens sometimes, but that's because we live in a democracy. You can't decide things on your own. You have to work with other politicians. I think that one of the biggest problems in our society today is that people aren't interested enough in politics. Everybody says I can't change anything so I won't try. Lots of people don't even vote.
Emma: Well, I would vote if I was old enough. At least I would vote if I knew who to vote for. But I don't think it makes so much difference really.
James: So how would you make things better?
Emma: I'm going to be a singer.
James: A singer?
Emma: Yes, I'm going to sing songs about how to treat each other. Music can change the world.
James: Oh, dream on, Emma.

a) Emma … 3. has read about violent school gangs in the paper.   5. is shocked that teenagers have been killed by other teenagers.
James … 2. is in a political youth group.   6. wants to be Prime Minister one day.
b) (1) council,   (2) campaigns,   (3) have to,   (4) hanging around,   (5) politicians,   (6) democracy
c) 2.

2 Reading: Queen of the United Kingdom, Canada, Australia, New Zealand and many more

a) Elizabeth II – who she is and what she does
Queen of: the United Kingdom (England, Scotland, Wales, Northern Ireland), Canada, Australia, New Zealand, Jamaica, the Bahamas, Barbados, Grenada, St Christopher and Nevis, St Lucia, the Solomon Islands, Tuvalu, St Vincent and the Grenadines, Papua New Guinea, Antigua, Barbuda and Belize
Head of State of: Great Britain, Australia, Canada
job is done by: Governor-General (Australia and Canada)

duties/tasks: open Parliament, sign laws, sign legal documents with other countries (GB); officially name Governor-General (Australia)
at opening of Parliament: the Queen reads Speech from the Throne (in GB and sometimes in Australia)
visits: Australia for important events, (Olympics, Australia Day), Canada visit regularly, have houses/palaces there

b) In GB the Queen is the Head of State. She can open and dissolve Parliament and she can decide not to sign legal documents and laws but she never does this. She has similar powers in Australia and she also officially names the Governor-General of Australia but she does not choose him or her.

c) Many Australians do not want to have the Queen as their Head of State. In 1999 only 54% of the population there voted to keep her. In Canada most people like the idea of having a queen, but many do not know that she is also their Head of State. It is only in French-speaking areas like Quebec that the Queen is not very popular.

3 Writing: The Royal Family

Lösungsvorschlag:
I think that the Royal Family should have to do normal jobs like everyone else. That way they would be closer to normal people and understand what life is like for a lot of people. Most people don't have a lot of money, and if they saw that every day, they wouldn't spend so much money on unimportant things, and maybe they wouldn't have as many houses and palaces, which cost a lot of money. Perhaps they would try to help poor people more.
OR:
I don't think that the Royal Family should have to do normal jobs. They get a lot of money from the state, but they work very hard. The Queen does a lot of charity work, and has a full-time job really, even though she is over 80 years old. The Royal Family is very important for Britain because they are also very important to tourists. That means that the country earns a lot of money because of the Royal Family. I think they improve the image Britain has in the world. If they had normal jobs, they wouldn't be able to do as much work in public.

4 Modal auxiliaries

1. Am I allowed to ask
2. has to read, have to bring
3. was able to have, was also able to have
4. had to open
5. Is she allowed to change, is not allowed to stop

5 Passive

1. The Queen of England was crowned in 1952.
2. Famous people are sometimes invited to lunch by the Queen.
3. The Queen is called 'Queen of Australia' by the Australians.
4. A new hospital was opened by the Queen last week.
5. Since 1952 over 387,700 awards and honours have been presented by her.
6. 'The Speech from the Throne' is written by the government.
7. Canada has been visited regularly by the Queen.
8. Her afternoons are devoted to her social duties.

6 Mixed bag

have, are given, represent, devote, collecting, can, was killed, joined, were demonstrating, attacked

7 Word puzzle

1. corridor;   2. occasionally;   3. antisocial;
4. innocent;   5. peaceful;   6. husband;
7. dislike;   8. cloudy;   9. confidential;
10. illegal;   11. likely;   12. launch;   13. daily

8 Find the word pairs

1. anti-social;   2. make bail;   3. seat belt;
4. chat room;   5. tear gas;   6. key player;
7. mustard seed;   8. prime minister;
9. sign up;   10. voting station

9 The world as a good place

member, hang around, majority, constructive, generation, misrepresented, aim, join, Sign up, campaign

10 Listening: Teenage Heroes!

Text:

Lucy: Hi, everyone, thanks for coming to our first meeting for the Teenage Heroes! campaign. It's a great turnout, and perhaps even more people will join us when they hear what we're doing. Right, my name's Lucy, and I want to start this campaign so that people will see what young people are really like, and what we can do. So what I'd like is for us to do lots of things to help the community and make this town and this area a better place. I think it would be best if we heard all your suggestions first and then we can decide who does what, OK? OK, so let's hear your ideas.

Emma: Umm, hi, I'm Emma, and I hate it that the countryside around here would be so beautiful if people didn't just throw their rubbish down everywhere. The river is full of old bikes and broken stuff and just rubbish.

Lucy: OK, so you would like to clean up the river – is that what you're saying?

Emma: Well, yeah, it would be a good start.

Lucy: Great, so is anyone else interested in helping – OK, great. So I'll call you Group A. OK, any more suggestions?

Rod: There's an old lady in my street. She can't walk very well, and she hasn't got anybody. Maybe she'd like some help. You know, we could do the shopping for her or clean her windows, I don't know.

Lucy: Yeah, what about giving help to more local pensioners? I bet they'd be glad if they had some help. Who wants to do that? Great, great. OK, you are all Group B. OK, who's next?

Julie: What about a campaign to encourage more people to ride bikes instead of using their cars all the time. The majority of people know that cars are bad for the environment, but they're too lazy. Perhaps we could somehow make it more fun for them to ride bikes.

Lucy: OK, anyone else interested in that? OK, two of you. Well, you'll need to think of ideas of how to do it, but I'm going to call you Group C. Right …

Robert: Er … I'm in a drama group and I think it would be great to perform a show at the jail, for example …

Lucy: The jail?! Hey, I never thought of that – good idea!

Robert: Yeah, they probably don't have a great life in there, so I thought …

Lucy: Yeah, who wants to do that with … er …

Robert: Robert.

Lucy: With Robert? Hey, wow! Right, you're all Group D.

Sadie: My neighbour's little girl is in kindergarten, and they've only got a small playground. What about building an adventure playground for them?

Lucy: Hey, what great ideas! Yeah, I like that. Anyone interested? Great! OK, you're Group E. So, any more ideas?

1E; 2A; 3B; 4D; 5C

11 Speaking: Car-free zone

You: Hello, would you mind not driving down this street today?

You: Well, it's part of the Teenage Heroes! campaign. We want people to ride bikes more often, especially in the town centre.

You: Well, we did give people warning, sir. There have been ads on the radio every day since Tuesday.

You: Well, I'm sorry about that, but there are signs everywhere near the town centre, too.

You: Yes, there's one over there. I think you drove past it.

You: Well, I'm (your name) and we're a group of teenagers who are trying to improve the town and the countryside. We're doing lots of different activities this week.

You: Thank you.

12 Writing: Change

Individuelle Schülerlösungen

13 Mediation: Skateistan

1. 2
2. *Es geht um eine Schule in Kabul in Afghanistan, in der Skateboarding und andere Fächer unterrichtet werden. Sie bitten um Spenden, um die Schule am Laufen halten zu können.*
3. *Es gehen 320 Schüler dahin.*
4. *Einige der Kinder arbeiten den ganzen Tag auf Kabuls Straßen seit sie sieben oder acht Jahre alt sind.*
5. *Sie haben einen kurzen Dokumentarfilm, der "To Live and Skate Kabul" heißt, gesehen und das Skateistan-Projekt dadurch entdeckt.*
6. *Sie brauchen Geld für Schulausrüstung, Essen und Transport für die Schüler, Organisationskosten und Unterkunft für die freiwilligen internationalen Lehrer und Lehrerinnen.*
7. *Der schnellste und einfachste Weg ist über PayPal, aber die effektivste Methode ist, das Geld direkt auf das Konto von Skateistan in Kabul zu überweisen.*

Zusätzlicher Text für das Hörverstehen: Reasons why teenagers vote

Wendy: This is WKTR Radio and my name is Wendy Rosenberg. Today I am live in Madison, Wisconsin. This is home to the University of Wisconsin-Madison and it is also the state capital. But we're not here to see the sights. Today I want to find out about the role of young adults in US politics and to do that I'm going to ask young adults what they think. Excuse me. Do you have time to answer a question for me?

YA1: Yeah, sure.

Wendy: In the 2008 presidential election, there were very high numbers of young and first-time voters. 24 million voters aged 18 to 29 went to vote – the highest number since the early 1970s. What do you think was the reason for this?

YA1: Well, hey, it was a very exciting election. It was a great time to be a part of a democracy. The candidates had real messages that represented what was important to us. And the candidate, well, the one I voted for, he … okay, I voted for Obama. Well, Obama really knows how to motivate people. A lot of his campaign was on the Internet. That's perfect for young people.

Wendy: In fact, two thirds of the young adults voted for Obama in 2008.

YA1: Oh, I believe that. He's not a stereotype, not a normal politician. He made us hopeful that as the head of government he could change a lot of things that the previous president did wrong. He sent out a call for action, especially to the young people. And I think so many young people voted in the election for him because they wanted to share his vision. Yeah, that's why.

Wendy: Are you involved in politics?

YA1: Yeah, there's a real need for young people in politics. My aim is to be in the Wisconsin State Senate … well, someday. You know …

Wendy: That's great. Thanks for answering my question and I hope you'll achieve your goal.
In 2010 there was another election in the US. This time it wasn't for the president but for the Congress. These politicians represent their home states in Washington, D.C. The turnout of young people was not as high this time. Let's find out why. Hello, I have some questions about politics. Do you have time to answer them?

YA2: Well, OK. What do you want to ask?

Wendy: Why do you think the turnout of young voters was so much lower[1] in 2010 than in 2008?

YA2: Oh, you mean the elections for Congress. It just didn't seem as important as 2008. And I didn't know most of the candidates.

Wendy: So you didn't vote in 2010?

YA2: No, the topics didn't really have anything to do with my daily life. I guess you could say they lacked a real message. In 2008 everyone was talking about the election and it was all over the Internet. That's where I got a lot of my information. But in 2010 … well, there just wasn't anything there. Nothing to keep my interest. No candidate or topic really emerged as, as something that made you say "wow".

Wendy: Do you think the majority of young adults shares your view?

YA2: Well, I can only speak for my friends, you know people I really know. And yeah, I think, well, I know that most of them didn't vote. I know people who

joined political parties[2] in 2008 and in 2010 they just didn't vote.
Wendy: That's very interesting. Do you …

[1]low – *niedrig*, [2]party – *hier: Partei*

Zusätzlicher Text für das Leseverstehen:
May a queen wear the same dress twice?

Some Canadians were surprised last year when the Queen wore a 'recycled dress' to a dinner in Toronto, as reported in a newspaper. She had already worn the dress once before – on the island country of Trinidad and Tobago the autumn before. For some the dress, decorated with Swarovski crystals[1], was very social and for others very anti-social. Some believe it demonstrates that the Queen is worried about the hard economic times and is showing her sympathy. On the other hand[2], another newspaper asked the question whether the Queen was really interested in spending less money when they saw her with a pair of 3D glasses especially made for her. The glasses have the letter 'Q' formed by Swarovski crystals on the sides. What message does this send? It appears that royalty[3] can't go completely without a little bling[4].

This 'bling' can also be in the form of transport, for example. Some years Prince Charles' trips cost the British almost £1 million. One trip alone to Australia, New Zealand and Fiji cost almost £300,000. One reason that the trips are so expensive is how the royal family travels. They often don't use normal planes. They use private planes that transport only them and the people travelling with them. Or they take helicopters, Air Force planes or use the special royal 9-car train, which costs the British £900,000 a year. One MP said that using the royal train occasionally, about 15-20 times a year, does not give reason for the amount. And a £20 cinema ticket becomes much more expensive when Prince Charles spends almost £3,000 flying to London to watch the film. Some say the monarchs are undermining the British people.

Are transport costs the reason that the British monarchy is the most expensive in Europe? This is certainly not the only reason although they could save money in this area. The Windsors are a large family. One of the most expensive things is keeping the royal family safe. Some guess that over £50 million is spent on royal safety each year – a number some say would be much lower with just an elected president to protect. Another area which uses a lot of money is the many homes that the family maintains. Each castle and house needs people who take care of it the whole year. About £15 million are spent on living quarters each year – workers, repairs, decorations.

The BBC reported that the royal family cost each British who pays taxes 61p each year. People who support the monarchy think that this is a good deal, that the monarchy is very valuable for the money it costs. The royal family does a lot of charity work, is good for Britain's image and is especially good for the number of tourists. Their effect should not be undervalued.

A man who used to work for the Windsor family disagrees with this and said, "The Windsors are very good at working three days a week, five months of the year and making it look as though[5] they work hard." Maybe in the future the Queen will have to work a little harder so that she doesn't have to recycle her dresses as she represents Britain around the world. But really, would the majority of tourists even notice that the Queen was wearing the same dress for the second time?

[1]crystal – *Kristall*, [2]on the other hand – *auf der anderen Seite*, [3]royalty – *Königlichkeit*, [4]bling – *Klunker*, [5]as though – *als ob*

Topic 3

1 Listening: On holiday in India

Text:

Rickshaw driver: Come over here. Where would you like to go? I can take you anywhere.
Woman: We'd like to go to the station. How much will it cost?
Rickshaw driver: That'll be 20 rupees.
Woman: 20? But it only cost ten rupees yesterday.
Rickshaw driver: But look at the traffic today. It'll take twice as long as it took yesterday.
Man: We'll pay ten or we'll go to your friend over there.
Rickshaw driver: Ten? Do you want to take the food from my children's mouths? I'll take you for 16.
Man: Twelve.
Rickshaw driver: OK, get in.
Woman: You know: I don't like all that haggling. We've just saved eight rupees. How much is that? Ten pence? It's nothing for us but it would buy that man something to eat.
Man: Yes, but it's normal. Everybody does it. People expect you to haggle. He enjoyed it.
Woman: He'd have enjoyed it more if we'd paid him twenty rupees. He'd have been able to give his children some more to eat.
Man: He probably hasn't got any children. You know people tell all kinds of lies just to get your money.
Woman: Oh, we don't know that's true. People probably say that just to make themselves feel better. 'I'm not giving my money to that poor man because he's just lying to me. He's probably got thousands in the bank'. That makes it easy. But anyway, I think I'd lie if I really needed the money. Yes! If I was hungry, I'd lie. It's as easy as that.
Man: Yes OK. You're right. So would I. I'd lie to feed myself or anybody in my family. But if you pay too much for something, it causes a real problem. If all the tourists, for example, who come to India pay more for things like rickshaw rides, then the prices go up. That means that people who live here can't afford them.
Woman: Er? What?
Man: If we – and other tourists – pay 20 rupees for a journey that normally costs 10 rupees, then rickshaw drivers will always ask for 20 rupees. That means that many Indians will not be able to afford to take a rickshaw.
Woman: But wouldn't the rickshaw driver then be able to pay more money for things? And that would mean that he could buy more. Then other people would have more money so everybody would be richer. Wouldn't they?
Man: Oh, I don't know, Diane. It's complicated, isn't it? I mean people study the economy, don't they?
Woman: Yes, it's complicated so …
Rickshaw driver: OK. We're here. That's twelve rupees, please.
Man: Here you are.
Rickshaw driver: Oh, thank you, sir. Thank you. That's very kind of you.
Man: You're welcome.
Woman: You gave him 20 rupees, didn't you?
Man: I did not. That would make the prices …
Woman: Oh, yes you did.

a) the woman: 1., 5.;   the man: 2., 4., 5.
b) the station, the traffic, ten rupees, children's mouths, 16 rupees
c) 1. right;   2. wrong;   3. wrong;   4. right;
   5. right;   6. wrong;   7. right;   8. right

2 Reading: The Indian fashion industry

a) Cotton goes round the world: B
   Early beginnings of cotton: A
   Working children: D
   Beautiful saris: E
   Factory production: C
b) 2., 4., 5., 8.
c) earn less, allowed to work, work illegally, less than adults, people are trying, to feed all their children, all day long, Older children, have no chance
d) 1. c;   2. a;   3. e;   4. b;   5. f;   6. d

3 Reporting

how to book a safari, he wanted to see elephants and tigers, to call him, she had to go to hospital, would go with her, he would come back tonight, I could only let her have a room for two nights, would take the room, had to go out, wouldn't be back until late, to buy a nice sari for his wife, was not too expensive, my cousin had a shop

4 Listening: Indian dance

Text:

Jane: Good morning, listeners. Today our topic is India and we're going to talk about the latest books by Indian authors and about Bollywood films. But before we get to that, I want to talk to Mani Jaffri, who is here in the studio with me. Mani is the organizer of a huge 'Festival of Indian Dance'. After a tour of Europe, its first performance in Britain is tomorrow night at the O2 arena. Is that correct, Mani?

Mani: Good morning, Jane. Yes, that is correct. The Festival of Indian Dance will be at the O2 for a week. The performance starts at 7:30 every evening and there will be an extra show on Saturday afternoon, starting at 2:30 pm. It is a very colourful show, and it's great entertainment.

Jane: Yes, Mani has brought along some photographs of some of the dancers. Some of the women are wearing beautiful saris in bright colours and with lots of gold. And in another picture there's a group of men. If I can describe them for our listeners: they're wearing bright yellow trousers and pink shirts and they have bright blue scarves round their waists. Can you tell us what it is they're wearing on their heads, Mani?

Mani: Of course. It is a kind of scarf and they wear it like a cap. You will also see in the picture that the dancers carry small drums. These are traditional for this type of dance, which comes from Eastern India. As you can see, these are all young men: they have to be young and very fit to perform this dance, because they play the drum and sing and dance all at the same time. It is a very exciting dance to watch.

Jane: I can imagine! And I can see in the photograph that the dancers' feet are not on the ground: all the dancers are leaping into the air. But this is a men's dance …

Mani: Yes, that's true. Its origins are in war dances, so it is danced by men.

Jane: I imagine the women's dances are quite different.

Mani: Yes, of course. India is a huge country with many different languages and religions and of course each area has different traditions. Some dances started as religious dances. I think this is sometimes difficult for people in the West to understand.

Jane: Yes, right. Although if we go back to our very old traditions they include religious dances, too, and dances that tell a story.

Mani: Ah, yes, that is important! Most types of traditional or, as we now call it, 'classical Indian dance' include telling a story through the dance, and that means singing and acting <u>and</u> dancing.

Jane: Mani, I'm sure that many of our listeners are familiar with Bollywood films, and we're going to be talking about Bollywood later in the programme. Those films include singing, dancing and acting. How different is the dancing that we see in Bollywood films from the 'classical', traditional dances that you're presenting in the 'Festival of Indian Dance'?

Mani: Well, of course the movements are similar, but we are presenting the original, traditional form of the dances, in the traditional costumes. What you see in Bollywood films has been influenced by Western dance, especially by musicals.

Jane: Well, I'm sure we'll hear more about that when we talk about Bollywood films later in the programme. In the meanwhile, thank you to Mani Jaffri for telling us about the Festival of Indian Dance at the O2 arena from tomorrow. And after that, where can our listeners see it, Mani?

Mani: After London it will tour to Birmingham, Manchester, Cardiff, Newcastle and Edinburgh.

Jane: Thank you. Now, on to books by Indian writers …

a) 1B, 2A, 3B, 4A, 5C, 6A, 7C
b) The movements are the same, but Bollywood dancing is more Western.
Traditional dancing is like the original dances with traditional costumes.

5 Odd one out

1. cotton; 2. sari; 3. fur; 4. currency; 5. vegetarian; 6. superpower

6 Opposites

1. dawn; 2. low; 3. simple/easy; 4. ally

7 How do you say it?

●••/●•••	•●•/•●••	••●•/••●••
backpacker complicated currency emperor	compartment religious selection	engineering independence vegetarian

8 India after 1947

independence, campaign, soul, peaceful, violence, soldiers, allies, religious, area, struggle

9 Writing: Children in India

Lösungsvorschlag:
Families want their children to work because they are poor and need the money. Parents do not have enough money to feed their family so they send the children to work in factories or on farms. Some children stay at home and work; they are paid to do simple jobs for many hours a day.
Many of these children work in the textile industry. India has a very large textile industry which exports clothes to many countries around the world. By using cheap child labour the industry can make sure its products are not too expensive. However, this causes big problems for the children. The young workers cannot go to school, and many become sick and die because they have to do a lot of hard physical work.

10 Writing: Making a protest

Lösungsvorschlag:
Dear Sir or Madam,
I am writing to your newspaper about the problem of child labour in India. It is a fact that many children in India have to work hard every day to earn their living. I ask myself: What can we do here in our country to help these children? We can start by finding out which clothes companies have children in their factories. Then we can stop buying products from these companies. In general we should try to buy things that are not made by children. We can also support organizations that help poor families and their children lead a better life. Another idea would be to help charities that set up schools for poor children. I hope these ideas are useful.
Yours faithfully,
…

11 Speaking: About India

Individuelle Schülerlösungen

12 Mediation: Indian fashion

You: *Da steht, dass die Filmschauspielerinnen oft Kleider aus Sari-Stoff tragen, der wunderschöne Goldborten hat.*
You: *Da steht, dass die Modekleider zwar auf Saris basieren, aber anders hergestellt werden.*
You: *Das ist eine Beschreibung der „kurta". Das ist ein indisches Hemd, das bei der Hitze besonders bequem ist. Es ist ein weit geschnittenes Baumwollhemd mit loser Passform und es ist in vielen Farben und Mustern erhältlich. In einem einfachen frischen Weiß sieht es besonders cool aus.*

Zusätzlicher Text für das Hörverstehen: Life in a slum

Street worker: How long have you lived in a slum?
Young man: I've lived here all my life. I was born here in the slum.
Street worker: And what about your parents' arrival in the slum?
Young man: I think it's a typical story. They moved from a rural area to the big city. They wanted to make more money. But they couldn't afford a flat. So they found this slum and at first they could hardly afford it. But now it's home.
Street worker: You call it home, just like more than half of the population of Mumbai call a slum their home. But for outsiders that's hard to understand. Slums are seen as terrible places.
Young man: Well, but the slum is not corrupt – like the politicians in the city. The slum is crowded, but it's usually peaceful. I mean, the city is really full, too, but it doesn't have any of this peace; it's an aggressive place. People from outside see a slum as a, like a jungle, but we are organized. We share responsibilities, for example: there are areas that we must keep clean together. There are leaders in the slum who organize the people and the duties. The leaders are very respected people.
Street worker: What happens when new people come to the slum?

Young man: They must go to one of the leaders. It matters what kind of person it is and if there's room for the person and their family. The leader will say yes or no to the person. If he says yes, he will say which house they can have. The new people must show that they can afford to care for their house. The leaders have got a lot of – what do you say? – influence, you know.

Street worker: That's interesting. But what about you? Are you going to leave the slum? Your English is very good.

Young man: Oh, thank you. Yes, I'm … umm … I'm optimistic that one day I will leave the slum. I don't want to only survive; I want to live.

Street worker: What will you do when you leave the slum?

Young man: Well, now I already work a lot with tourists. I help them to find a hotel or a room. They like it when I speak English to them. It makes them feel safe. My real dream is to work in Bollywood. I know people there and they say I can get work there soon. Then I will leave the slum. Look, life in the slum is hard, everything is a struggle. It is very hard to get medicine, for example. Often we must buy it from the black market and it is very difficult to find a doctor who will come to the slum to help.

Street worker: Is it unusual for people to leave the slum?

Young man: No, no it's not unusual, in fact it is quite common. Most of the people in the slums have the belief that they will have a better life someday. And they work very hard; they save every rupee that they can. I mean look, there are even people who live in the slum and they have jobs in offices in the city. Maybe they just have to stay a little longer and save a little more and then they can do it. They can leave the slum. But yes, I mean there are people who will always live here. If they, you know, don't have a regular income. Then they have to take any job they can get and sometimes if it's like a construction job, it's only for a short time. The economy … uh … does things … I mean has an influence on our lives, too. If they are building many things in the city, then we can earn more, too.

Street worker: What kind of people live in slums?

Young man: It's like I already said – many different kinds of people. Just normal people. We celebrate weddings and births and have deaths in the slums, too. The network in a slum is very important. With the network you know who can do what, who can help with which problems. Like that. You know, because we have to look after ourselves. No politicians ever come to the slums. We don't have many rights. But, you know, a slum is unlike any other place you will ever live.

Zusätzlicher Text für das Leseverstehen: India and its animals

The endangered tiger is perhaps the national animal of India, but there are two other animals that also play large roles.

The first animal is the cow. The cow is important because of its role in the Hindu religion. There are about 900 million Hindus in the world and most of them live in India. In the Hindu religion, respecting animals is a main theme and their belief is that cows are holy[1]. This is perhaps the most known fact about Hinduism worldwide. Some say this goes back to the god Krishna who is sometimes described as 'a child who protects the cows'. The cow is also seen as the mother of all cultures and its milk the food. In fact, milk is often used in Hindu religious ceremonies. People think it brings them good luck to give a cow a piece of bread or fruit before breakfast and you can be sent to prison for killing or hurting a cow.

Cows in India are allowed to walk wherever they want to. Unfortunately, this includes city streets, which has become a problem. In densely populated Delhi, for example, 13 million people share the streets with about 40,000 cows. Some people complain that the cows spread² rubbish around the city when they rip open rubbish bags, looking for food. A more dangerous problem is cows in traffic, which can cause traffic jams³ and even worse, accidents. One journalist jokingly suggested that cows be given "reflectors and, if not number plates⁴, at least passports."

The city is trying to do something about the cow problem without disrespecting the Hindu community. Delhi has about 100 modern cowboys, or cow catchers, who try to take them to a location outside the city and sometimes even to special cow parks. The work isn't easy. The cows can hurt the cowboys with their sharp horns⁵ and the cows aren't dumb either. Sometimes the cows still find their way back into the city after they have been taken away.

The other important Indian animal, which can also be seen in cities, is the elephant. Elephants have played an important role in Indian culture and religious life for hundreds of years. Almost 60% of all wild elephants in Asia live in India. Of course hundreds of years ago the actual number of elephants in India was much higher than it is today. Scientists have guessed that in the early 17th century there were probably more than 1 million wild elephants in India. Today those numbers are much lower for one main reason: the elephants are losing the land that they live on because the human population is increasing and needs more land to live on and for farms.

In 1992 an organization called Project Elephant was formed. One goal is to save the elephants' land and make elephant "corridors" for wild elephants. These are like paths between the areas where the elephants live because elephants travel from one area to another. Project Elephant was able to found 25 protected areas for elephants.

Another goal is to improve the situation of elephants who live with private people. Privately owned elephants are in temples, zoos, circuses, the forest department⁶ and in private homes. With the exception of the elephants in the forest department, the animals are almost always kept for financial reasons (to make money) and are often not well cared for. Even temple elephants are kept to increase profits and some are kept in one spot with a chain their whole lives. Elephants are used to give rides to tourists in crowded areas and are often overwhelmed by the hard, long work.

¹holy – *heilig*, ²to spread, spread, spread – *verteilen*,
³traffic jam – *Stau*, ⁴number plate – *Nummernschild*,
⁵sharp horns – *spitze Hörner*, ⁶department – *hier: Behörde*

Topic 4

1 Listening: Talking about the future

Text:

Anneena: You aren't really going to leave school at the end of this year, are you?
William: Yes, I am. I'm going to go and work for my dad.
Anneena: Are you? That sounds dangerous.
William: Dangerous? Why?
Anneena: Well, I wouldn't like to work for my dad. We'd argue all the time and fight.
William: Yes, I think it could be difficult, but my dad wants me to know and understand everything about his company, so that I can have it when he's too old.
Anneena: And do you want it?
William: Well, I don't really know. My older brother and sister didn't want to work for my dad and he was really disappointed. I'm the youngest and if I don't go into my dad's company, he'll have to sell it when he gets too old. That would break his heart.
Anneena: What does your dad's firm do?
William: They make things out of metal.
Anneena: Wouldn't it be better if you went to college and got some qualifications before you worked for your dad?
William: Well, my dad doesn't think so. He left school when he was 15 and he's been very successful.
Anneena: But what would you like to do?
William: I'd like to go to college and do art but my parents are really against it. They say that it's very difficult for artists to earn enough money.
Anneena: That's true, I suppose. But you're really good at art. I think your parents should let you do what you want. It's your life.
William: Yes, you're right, but they say I'm not old enough to decide myself.
Anneena: And what do you think?
William: I think that I'd like to try working for my dad and then if I don't like it, I can leave. Then my parents can't say that I never tried.
Anneena: I suppose that's a good idea but you're just wasting your life. And it'll be more difficult to go to college when you're older, won't it?
William: No, I don't think so. Both my brother and my sister changed their minds when they were older. My brother

started studying at university but then left before he finished. He went to work in Africa for a while. And my sister started work when she was 16 but then stopped and went to a college of further education. – But what about you? Are you still going to go to Sixth Form College?

Anneena: Yes, I am. I have to do my A levels so that I can go to university and study to be a doctor.

William: That will take a long time, won't it? Another seven or eight years? I don't think I'd like that either.

Anneena: Well, it could be hard. But it could be great fun, too.

William: Your dad's a doctor, isn't he?

Anneena: Yes, there are lots of doctors in my family. Most people who grow up in India think that's one of the best jobs you can have.

William: Is that why you want to be a doctor?

Anneena: No! OK, I suppose it must have some influence on my decision.

William: And what would you like to do if you didn't want to become a doctor?

Anneena: I'd like to study sport and play football, but …

William: No, don't tell me. I know. Your parents don't like you playing football.

Anneena: Well …

a) 1. wrong; 2. wrong; 3. right; 4. right; 5. wrong; 6. right
b) 1. c; 2. a; 3. e; 4. b; 5. d
c) 1B, 2A, 3C, 4C, 5B, 6B

2 Reading: Salford College

a) 1. Try different internships or choose an introduction course.
   2. Decide on your career.
   3. Decide on the level.
   4. Decide on the course.
   5. Get the application form.
   6. Fill it in.
   7. Wait to be called for interview.

b) <u>Find interesting</u>: get to learn about different areas of business; gain practical experience by doing a placement in a business
<u>Why this course</u>: think it is good that during the course you can concentrate on the part of business which you are most interested in
<u>Why I am right for this course:</u> I am very good at Maths and English; I am good with computers

3 Writing: An application

Lösungsvorschlag:
I want to do the Business Studies course at Salford College because I think it is a very interesting course. The course will give me the chance to learn about the different areas of business. I also want to gain practical experience by doing a placement in a real business. Once I have decided which area of business really interests me, I will then be able to concentrate on this area while I am doing the course. I think I would do well on this course because I am good at Maths and English. I have also worked a lot with computers, so I would be interested in doing extra qualifications in IT during the course.

4 What people should do

Lösungsvorschlag:
1. I think she should talk to her parents. It is important that they know what is happening so that they can help her. Then they should go see a doctor so they can make sure that Jessie and the baby are healthy. Then they could go to an advice centre to talk about the situation and get help.
2. I think he should go tell his parents about the money and the motorcycle. He should tell his parents that he will pay them back. Then Matt and his parents will have to go talk to his neighbour. Matt must figure out a way to pay his neighbour back for all the damage. Then they will all have to go talk to the police.
3. I think Don should tell his parents about the exam. Then Don and his parents should go talk to his teacher. Finally, Matt should tell his friend the truth.

5 Writing: Giving advice

Lösungsvorschläge:
1. Dear Robert, You should go talk to your parents. They may not be aware of the problems that you are having. You could also think about talking to a teacher at your school. Maybe you have a teacher that you feel would understand and might be able to help. The important thing is that you talk to someone and get help. Yours, Christopher
2. Dear Molly, It sounds as if you and your friend both have a drinking problem. You both need to talk to someone about your problem and get help. You could start by talking to your parents or see if there is anyone you could talk to at school or at a local youth centre. Yours, Christopher

3. Dear Cathy, You should talk to your parents. They need to know what is happening so that they can help you. This is a difficult situation which you should not have to deal with alone. Yours, Agony Angel

4. Dear Ben, Have you tried talking to your parents about the situation at home. They may not be aware of how you feel. Maybe together you can find ways to improve things. Perhaps making a few positive changes can help everyone in the family. Yours, Agony Angel

6 Listening: Where are they?

Text:

1. Mr Pearl: Now, tell me, Mr Jenkins, why do you want this job?
   Tom: Well, I think it sounds really interesting, because it's about going out and talking to people, not just sitting in an office all day.
   Mr Pearl: You will have to do a bit of office work, you know.
   Tom: Yes, of course. There's always paperwork. I don't mind that. But can you tell me how big an area I would have to cover? I mean, how many customers I could expect to look after.
   Mr Pearl: Not exactly, at the moment. You see, we're going to make two areas out of the West Midlands. It's too big for one person to cover …

2. Woman: I like this brown one, but the green one is nice, too.
   Salesgirl: Both those colours look good on you. And the brown looks great with the trousers you're wearing.
   Woman: That's why I'm not sure. I don't wear this colour very often.
   Salesgirl: You could wear either of those with jeans and they'd both look great with black.
   Woman: Brown and black? Do you think so? I really don't know. I like the green one but I don't think that colour looks so good on me …

3. Boy: Let's see what they're showing this week. Hey, "Night Ghost" looks interesting.
   Girl: Hmmm. Is it a horror movie? I don't like horror movies. All those awful things they show give me a fright!
   Boy: Aw, come on! It's only a movie, it's not real!
   Girl: Yes, but it looks real. How about "The Italian Girl"? That looks nice.
   Boy: What is it? Oh, it says "A story of love lost and found in the romantic setting of one of Italy's most beautiful cities." Oh yuk. That sounds really awful.
   Girl: I suppose you want something with a lot of noise and guns and fast cars. Well I don't like …

4. Manager: One of your main jobs will be collecting the used cups and things from the tables. It's important to keep the tables clean, customers don't like to find the tables all dirty.
   Girl: Well, that doesn't seem difficult. Where do I put the used cups?
   Manager: Take them out to the back. Throw away any empty sugar packets, things like that, and put the cups and plates in the dishwasher …

5. Girl: Dad, do you know a company called "GK supplies"?
   Dad: 'GK Supplies'? No, I don't think so. Why?
   Girl: Well, they've got an ad on the 'Jobs' website. They're looking for an office assistant who will work to the senior secretary and the orders department. What do they mean by that?
   Dad: That sounds like what we used to call 'the office junior'. They want someone to make the coffee, take messages, do the photocopying; do all the little odd jobs that other people haven't got time for.
   Girl: Oh, I don't like the sound of that. And anyway, I've just looked at the company's website and found out what it is they supply. No, I don't think I want to work for them.

A3, B1, C--, D2, E5, F4

7 Word box: In hospital

Across:
1. admit;   6. operation
Down:
1. anorexia;   2. mental;   3. illness;
4. doctor;   5. disease

8 Which word?

1. agriculture;   2. studies, horticulture;
3. wheelchair, operations, hospital;
4. illness, employment, are aware of;
5. self-employment, manage, difficulty

9 Writing: Advice to a friend

Lösungsvorschlag:
1. Hi Terry. Sorry can't give you number for Alicia. She will tell you if she wants to hear from you.
2. Hi Marie. I will come and bring you money for bus home. Tell me where you are and wait there. Don't speak to anyone!
3. Not on a school night, Jinx. Maths test tomorrow! Underground club too dark and loud for me. See you in school.

10 Speaking: Non-electronic-media week

Lösungsvorschlag:
For the idea: we are too dependent on electronic devices so we should try to live without them; have time for other things like sports; save money, for example, on mobiles; spend more time with family; will make life calmer
Against the idea: won't know what is happening in the world; can't stay in touch with friends; can't contact family in an emergency; will make life boring

11 Speaking: About India

Individuelle Schülerlösungen

12 Mediation: How school can help

You: … a social worker and two assistants … improve the situation for students.
You: … talk to students, teachers and parents.
You: … they can be in groups, too.
You: … they provide activities for students in their free time. … there's a special course about violence.
You: … students can put a note in the box to ask for help with a personal problem or a problem with friends or in class. … through conversations and meetings.

Zusätzlicher Text für das Hörverstehen: Talking about age limits

Kyle: "It's your hour"! This is Kyle Campbell. Welcome to the radio hour just for teenagers and young 20s. Our topic tonight is age limits. What's good, what's bad about age limits on things like working, voting and driving? What do you think? Have you had positive or negative experiences with age limits? Check out our website: www.radioone.com/itsyourhour We've got a grid with information on different age limits around the world. So call us or send us a message – it's your hour! And here's our first caller from Brooklyn. Hi there, caller. What's your name?

Pam: I'm Pam and I just wanted to say that, um, I'm 21 now, but when I was 16, I was dying to drive. Like everyone. And of course I got my driver's license. But when I look back now, there was no way that I should have been on the streets driving a car. I was not really prepared. I mean you have to make a lot of decisions while you're driving and I just don't think 16-year-old kids have the mental skills to do that. OK, that's all I wanted to say. Bye.

Kyle: Thanks, Pam. Now I've got an e-mail for you on a completely different subject. This is from Jack in Vancouver. He writes, "Dear Kyle, I've got a very strong opinion on voting. In Canada the official voting age is 18. I think it should be 16. When you are 16, you can drive, you can be employed and pay taxes and insurance. A lot of the government's decisions can change things in our lives, too. There's no voting age limit at the top. If you're 100, you can vote although in the near future things won't change much for you. But they will for teenagers! The government shouldn't deny this right to teenagers." Great to hear from you, Jack. In fact, the Canadian government was thinking about changing the voting age from 18 to 16. Send them a letter, Jack, so the government is aware of your opinion – because I don't think they're listening to "It's Your Hour". Here's a little music and then we'll talk some more. …

Kyle: Welcome back to "It's Your Hour". We're talking about age limits tonight. Our next call is from Clint. Where are you from Clint?

Clint: Uh, hi. Um, I'm from San Diego.

Kyle: And which age limit do you want to talk about?

Clint: Well, I think the age limit on buying alcohol is stupid. I mean, 21? Come on! I can have a job at 14, drive a car at 16, vote as well as get married at 18, but I can't buy any alcohol. So I couldn't even have alcohol when I get married! If I can make all those other decisions, then the government can hardly say I'm not sensible enough to buy alcohol.

Kyle: Don't you think there would be a rise in car accidents involving alcohol if it weren't illegal for teenagers?

Clint: That's a very common opinion, but I think it's wrong. I think there are so many accidents because it's illegal. The teenagers have to hide it, they can't drink alcohol where people can see. If it were out in the open, then, well, I think teens get the wrong message about alcohol. How can you learn to be responsible about something if it's illegal? I think if we could buy alcohol at 18 or even 17 it would prepare us more for, for, yeah, being adults and being responsible.

Kyle: Thanks so much for your call, Clint. Here's one more e-mail and it's about alcohol, too. Bruce from Orlando writes, "You can't let new drivers buy alcohol. The first milestone for teenagers is driving. Let them manage that first. There's plenty of time for alcohol later when they have become aware of the difficulties." Thanks, Bruce. Time for some more music.

Zusätzlicher Text für das Leseverstehen: Need some money?

Take out your wallet. Open it and look inside. What do you see? Do you have any money? Do you have enough money? If you're an ordinary teenager, the answers are probably yes and no. "Yes, I have some money" and "No, I don't have enough money." Have you ever thought about trying to change that? How about starting your own company to make your wallet fatter? Self-employment is often worth it for teenagers. It can be something as simple as a gardening business (many adults don't enjoy cutting their grass) or computer services (many teenagers know more about computers than adults). Or it could be something more difficult such as marketing and public relations services (especially if adults need help selling a product to young people) or manufacturing recyclable bags (young people often have excellent ideas). But how do you get there? How do you become your own boss?

The first step starts with you. Think about what you are interested in, what you know a lot about, which area you are an expert it. Do you maybe have a new idea about how to solve an old problem? Can you find a better way to do something? Write down all kinds of creative ideas and solutions. Try things out, think things out to the end, build a prototype. Be aware of the trends around you. Is there an idea for you there? Business is really about buying and selling. Are there enough people who will buy what you are selling? Think about the market around you.

After you have made a decision, in the second step you need to develop a plan. Your business plan should be as specific as possible with your expected milestones because this will help you to be more successful. First of all describe your business and your idea in detail. Include things like why you are better or different than the competition. How can you beat them? The second point is marketing. Describe who your customers will be and how you will contact them. The third point is finances. Explain where you will get money to start your business. Will you need a loan? Prepare a monthly and yearly financial plan. Write what kinds of sales you can expect. Make an assessment of when you can expect to start making money from your business. The last point in your business plan is explaining the daily processes[1]. Who is the boss? Who is responsible? Who makes which decisions?

In the third step you start building or preparing. Like a good house, your business also needs a basement, something to stand on. Make sure your business is well organized and that nothing about it is illegal. Do you need insurance? Following the laws will protect you as well as your customers. Your company and your product need names. These will be part of your image and your marketing strategy. What message do you want to send to your customers? You're a small business, but this also means you are flexible which can be a real advantage because you can change quickly to keep in front.

The next step is getting and keeping connected, finding links. You need to develop relationships with your customers, your bank, your employees and the people who manufacture or supply your product. Listen to advice, especially from other young people who are their own boss.

The last step is success – but this also takes skills, not just luck. Always have goals for yourself and your business. Don't just sit around. Get up and do something, lead! Don't be afraid to ask for help if you are having difficulties. Don't forget after-sales service. If you show your customers that you care, then they'll be certain to come back to you again. Learn from your mistakes and do it better the next time. Before long you will have reached[2] your goals!

[1] daily processes – *tägliche Prozesse*, [2] to reach – *erreichen*